Introduction to Humanities

Custom Edition for Florida SouthWestern State College

Taken from:
Perceiving the Arts: An Introduction to the Humanities, Tenth Edition
By Dennis J. Sporre

History of Art: The Western Tradition, Volume 1, Revised Sixth Edition,
by H.W. Janson and Anthony F. Janson

Writing About the Humanities, Third Edition
by Robert DiYanni

Fundamentals of Philosophy, Eighth Edition
by David Stewart, H. Gene Blocker, and James Petrik

Writing about Music: An Introductory Guide, Fourth Edition
by Richard J. Wingell

Cover Art: Courtesy of Pearson Learning Solutions.

Taken from:

Perceiving the Arts: An Introduction to the Humanities, Tenth Edition
By Dennis J. Sporre
Copyright © 2011, 2009, 2006, 2000 by Pearson Education, Inc.
Published by Prentice Hall
Upper Saddle River, New Jersey 07458

History of Art: The Western Tradition, Volume 1, Revised Sixth Edition,
by H.W. Janson and Anthony F. Janson
Copyright © 2004 by Pearson Education, Inc.
Published by Prentice Hall

Writing About the Humanities, Third Edition
by Robert DiYanni
Copyright © 2008, 2004, 2001 by Pearson Education, Inc.
Published by Prentice Hall

Fundamentals of Philosophy, Eighth Edition
by David Stewart, H. Gene Blocker, and James Petrik
Copyright © 2013, 2010, 2006 by Pearson Education, Inc.
Upper Saddle River, New Jersey 07458

Writing about Music: An Introductory Guide, Fourth Edition
by Richard J. Wingell
Copyright © 2009, 2002, 1997, 1990 by Pearson Education, Inc.
Published by Prentice Hall

Copyright © 2014 by Pearson Learning Solutions
All rights reserved.

Pearson Learning Solutions, 501 Boylston Street, Suite 900, Boston, MA 02116
A Pearson Education Company
www.pearsoned.com

Printed in the United States of America

4 16

000200010271863675

SR/SF

ISBN 10: 1-269-87130-7
ISBN 13: 978-1-269-87130-3

Contents

INTRODUCTION *1*

by Dr. Wendy Chase, Professor of
Humanities

CHAPTER 1

Why Study the Humanities *5*

Taken from: *Not For Profit: Why Democracy
Needs the Humanities*, by Nussbaum, Martha.
(Princeton: Princeton University Press,
2010)

CHAPTER 2

Music *11*

Writing About Music and Dance

Taken from: *Writing About the Humanities*,
Third Edition, by Robert DiYanni

How is it Put Together? *23*

Taken from: *Perceiving the Arts: An
Introduction to the Humanities*, Tenth Edition,
by Dennis J. Sporre

Questions to Consider *35*

Taken from: *Writing About Music: An
Introductory Guide*, Fourth Edition, by
Richard J. Wingell

CHAPTER 3

Visual Art *39*

Introduction to Art History

Taken from: *History of Art:
The Western Tradition*, Volume 1,
Revised Sixth Edition, by H.W. Janson
and Anthony F. Janson

History of Art: Primer of
Art History *49*

Taken from: *History of Art:
The Western Tradition*, Volume 1,
Revised Sixth Edition, by H.W. Janson
and Anthony F. Janson

CHAPTER 4

Architecture *57*

Writing About Art and Architecture

Taken from: *Writing About the Humanities*,
Third Edition, by Robert DiYan

Perceiving the Arts: Architecture *67*

Taken from: *Perceiving the Arts: An
Introduction to the Humanities*,
Tenth Edition, by Dennis J. Sporre

CHAPTER 5

Film   *99*

Writing About Film

Taken from: *Writing About the Humanities*,
Third Edition, by Robert DiYanni

Perceiving the Arts: Cinema   *113*

Taken from: *Perceiving the Arts:
An Introduction to the Humanities*,
Tenth Edition, by Dennis J. Sporre

CHAPTER 6

Literature   *133*

Taken from: *The Nature and Aim of
Fiction*, by O'Connor, Flannery.

CHAPTER 7

Theater   *143*

Taken from: *The Essential Theater*,
by Brockett, Oscar and Robert Ball.
(Cengage, 2011)

CHAPTER 8

Philosophy   *159*

Taken from: *Fundamentals of Philosophy*,
Eighth Edition, by David Stewart,
H. Gene Blocker, and James Petrik

Contents

INTRODUCTION *1*

by Dr. Wendy Chase, Professor of
Humanities

CHAPTER 1

Why Study the Humanities *5*

Taken from: *Not For Profit: Why Democracy
Needs the Humanities*, by Nussbaum, Martha.
(Princeton: Princeton University Press,
2010)

CHAPTER 2

Music *11*

Writing About Music and Dance

Taken from: *Writing About the Humanities*,
Third Edition, by Robert DiYanni

How is it Put Together? *23*

Taken from: *Perceiving the Arts: An
Introduction to the Humanities*, Tenth Edition,
by Dennis J. Sporre

Questions to Consider *35*

Taken from: *Writing About Music: An
Introductory Guide*, Fourth Edition, by
Richard J. Wingell

CHAPTER 3

Visual Art *39*

Introduction to Art History

Taken from: *History of Art:
The Western Tradition*, Volume 1,
Revised Sixth Edition, by H.W. Janson
and Anthony F. Janson

History of Art: Primer of
Art History *49*

Taken from: *History of Art:
The Western Tradition*, Volume 1,
Revised Sixth Edition, by H.W. Janson
and Anthony F. Janson

CHAPTER 4

Architecture *57*

Writing About Art and Architecture

Taken from: *Writing About the Humanities*,
Third Edition, by Robert DiYan

Perceiving the Arts: Architecture *67*

Taken from: *Perceiving the Arts: An
Introduction to the Humanities*,
Tenth Edition, by Dennis J. Sporre

iv   Contents

CHAPTER 5

Film   *99*

Writing About Film

Taken from: *Writing About the Humanities*,
Third Edition, by Robert DiYanni

Perceiving the Arts: Cinema   *113*

Taken from: *Perceiving the Arts:
An Introduction to the Humanities*,
Tenth Edition, by Dennis J. Sporre

CHAPTER 6

Literature   *133*

Taken from: *The Nature and Aim of
Fiction*, by O'Connor, Flannery.

CHAPTER 7

Theater   *143*

Taken from: *The Essential Theater*,
by Brockett, Oscar and Robert Ball.
(Cengage, 2011)

CHAPTER 8

Philosophy   *159*

Taken from: *Fundamentals of Philosophy*,
Eighth Edition, by David Stewart,
H. Gene Blocker, and James Petrik

Introduction

by Dr. Wendy Chase, Professor of Humanities

We live in an age of accelerated change where communities are radically redefined by the borderless parameters of cyberspace and the near-instantaneous transmission of information across cultures. As of 2012, over 4,000 books are published every day, one hundred hours of video are uploaded on YouTube every minute, and a new blog is created every second.[i] Technical information is currently changing so rapidly that half of what a student learns in a technical field their first year of college will be obsolete by the time they graduate.[ii] Educators across the disciplines struggle to determine what knowledge, skills and habits students need to acquire and develop in order to succeed in a professional climate that requires discriminating thought and adaptability to rapidly changing technology.

[i]Fisch, Karl and Scott McLeod. "Did You Know 2013?" shifthappens.wikispaces.com. Last modified Dec. 6, 2014. http://www.shifthappens.wikispaces.com.
[ii]ibid

What seems most apparent in this information economy is that students do not go to college merely to acquire more specialized information, although that is part of their process; they go to college to master the skills of critical and creative thinking so that they can use this specialized information effectively. This is why studying the humanities has historically been considered the cornerstone of a liberal arts education. Training in the humanities cultivates supple minds that can sift the trivial from the significant and apply the most useful information to whatever discipline a student is attempting to master. In addition to practicing critical and analytical thinking, studying the humanities also helps students synthesize material from multiple disciplines into an original idea, thereby fostering creative thinking as well.

Humanities courses are different from any other classes you take in college because they are interdisciplinary in nature. For example, you can't fathom the radical shift in painterly style that the Impressionists developed without studying Haussmann's renovation of Paris and the invention of photography. But once you understand Impressionism through painting, you can perceive echoes of this style in the music of Debussy, and see how it manifests in the writing of Virginia Woolf. As you weave together the connections between the influence of 19th century urban planning, photography, visual art, music and literature, your brain is being wired to think in terms of patterns, relationships and context. This is a valuable skill that trains us to become systemic problem-solvers who understand how interdependent parts function within a dynamic and complex system. These are skills that will serve you well whether you are studying to become an engineer, a video game programmer or human rights activist.

Knowledge tends to be compartmentalized on our college campuses; you are guided to take an ecology course one semester, an economics course the next, and perhaps some composition and speech courses sprinkled in along the way. And yet, if you are hired by an environmental engineering firm to solve some of the serious problems that we currently face, you must have an understanding of the relationship between ecology, economics, and a variety of other subjects in order to find a viable solution. Once you have identified the solution, you must be able to communicate a coherent plan to a diverse audience. Whereas math and science courses cultivate critical and creative thinking habits and English courses develop communication skills, humanities courses offer students a chance to activate all of these skills simultaneously as they contemplate the human experience.

While it is important to learn how to succeed in a dynamic professional landscape where information and technology are constantly evolving, it is equally important to realize that we are more than cogs in the economic machine and we want more than good jobs. Humans across time and cultures strive to construct meaningful lives led with purpose. But we can only achieve this goal if we shape and preserve communities populated by active, informed, and intelligent participants in a society based on respect for the experiences of others who are different from ourselves. The humanities train us to inhabit the perspective of other people in a variety of times and places. We may never have experienced random violence or poverty, but we can identify with Jamal in *Slumdog Millionaire*, or be moved by the music of Tupac Shakur. We might rethink our preconceptions of those who live within "the axis of evil" after reading the love poems of Rumi or watching the movies of Wong Kar-Wai. We can be inspired to combat the moral obtuseness that comes with group-speak by the words of Frederick Douglass, the lyrics of The Clash, or the Art of Ai Wei Wei. We might decide we want to learn how to give love rather than obsess over how we can get it after reading Rilke or listening to jazz. Ultimately, we might deepen our understanding of how our personal perspectives are informed by the cultural history of our families, our race, our nation and our world. What was true when Plutarch said it in the first century remains true in the twenty-first: "What we achieve inwardly will change outer reality." Prepare for a rewarding journey – both into your own hearts and minds and out into the world.

Why Study the Humanities

Reprinted from *Not for Profit: Why the Democracy Needs the Humanities* (2010), by permission of Princeton University Press.

Education is that process by which thought is opened out of the soul, and, associated with outward things, is reflected back upon itself, and thus made conscious of their reality and shape.

—BRONSON ALCOTT, MASSACHUSETTS EDUCATOR, C. 1850

[W]hile making use of [material possessions], man has to be careful to protect himself from [their] tyranny. If he is weak enough to grow smaller to fit himself to his covering, then it becomes a process of gradual suicide by shrinkage of the soul.

—RABINDRANATH TAGORE, INDIAN EDUCATOR, C. 1917

We are in the midst of a crisis of massive proportions and grave global significance. No, I do not mean the global economic crisis that began in 2008. At least then everyone knew that a crisis was at hand, and many world leaders worked quickly and desperately to find solutions. Indeed, consequences for governments were grave if they did not find solutions, and many were replaced in consequence. No, I mean a crisis that goes largely unnoticed, like a cancer; a crisis that is likely to be, in the long run, far more damaging to the future of democratic self-government: a worldwide crisis in education.

Radical changes are occurring in what democratic societies teach the young, and these changes have not been well thought through. Thirsty for national profit, nations, and their systems of education, are heedlessly discarding skills that are needed to keep democracies alive. If this trend continues, nations all over the world will soon be producing generations of useful machines, rather than complete citizens who can think for themselves, criticize tradition, and understand the significance of another person's sufferings and achievements. The future of the world's democracies hangs in the balance.

What are these radical changes? The humanities and the arts are being cut away, in both primary/secondary and college/university education, in virtually every nation of the world. Seen by policy-makers as useless frills, at a time when nations must cut away all useless things in order to stay competitive in the global market, they are rapidly losing their place in curricula, and also in the minds and hearts of parents and children. Indeed, what we might call the humanistic aspects of science and social science—the imaginative, creative aspect, and the aspect of rigorous critical thought—are also losing ground as nations prefer to pursue short-term profit by the cultivation of the useful and highly applied skills suited to profit-making.

This crisis is facing us, but we have not yet faced it. We go on as if everything were business as usual, when in reality great changes of emphasis are evident all over. We haven't really deliberated about these changes, we have not really chosen them, and yet they increasingly limit our future.

Consider these five examples, deliberately drawn from different nations and different educational levels:

- In the fall of 2006 the U.S. Department of Education's Commission on the Future of Higher Education, headed by Bush administration secretary of education Margaret Spellings, released its report on the state of higher education in the nation: *A Test of Leadership: Charting the Future of U.S. Higher Education.*[1] This report contained a valuable critique of unequal access to higher education. When it came to subject matter, however, it focused entirely on education for national economic gain. It concerned itself with perceived deficiencies in science, technology, and engineering—not basic scientific research in these areas, but only highly applied learning, learning that can quickly generate profit-making strategies. The humanities, the arts, and critical thinking were basically absent. By omitting them, the report strongly suggested that it would be perfectly all right if these abilities were allowed to wither away in favor of more useful disciplines.

- In March 2004 a group of scholars from many nations gathered to discuss the educational philosophy of Rabindranath Tagore—winner of the Nobel Prize for Literature in 1913, and leading innovator in education. Tagore's educational experiment, which had wide influence in Europe, Japan, and the United States, focused on the empowerment of the student through practices of Socratic argument, exposure to many world cultures, and, above all, the infusion of music, fine art, theater, and dance into every part of the curriculum. In India today, Tagore's ideas are neglected, and even scorned. Participants in the conference all agreed that a new conception, focused on profit, has taken over—in the process sidelining the whole idea of imaginative and critical self-development through which Tagore had formed so many future citizens of India's successful democracy. Would democracy in India survive today's assault upon its soul? Faced with so much recent evidence of bureaucratic obtuseness and uncritical group-think, many participants feared that the answer might be "No."

- In November 2005 a teachers retreat was held at the Laboratory School in Chicago—the school, on the campus of my own university, where John Dewey conducted his pathbreaking experiments in democratic education reform, the school where President Barack Obama's daughters spent their early formative years. The teachers had gathered to discuss the topic of education for democratic citizenship, and they considered a wide range of educational experiments, studying figures ranging from Socrates to Dewey in the Western tradition to the closely related ideas of Tagore in India. But something

was clearly amiss. The teachers—who take pride in stimulating children to question, criticize, and imagine—expressed anxiety about the pressures they face from wealthy parents who send their kids to this elite school. Impatient with allegedly superfluous skills, and intent on getting their children filled with testable skills that seem likely to produce financial success, these parents are trying to change the school's guiding vision. They seem poised to succeed.

- In fall 2005 the head of the search committee for the new dean of the School of Education at one of our nation's most prestigious universities called me for advice. Hereafter I will refer to the university as X. X's School of Education has enormous influence on teachers and schools all over the United States. As I began talking about the role of the humanities and arts in education for democratic citizenship, saying what I took to be familiar and obvious, the woman expressed surprise. "How unusual," she said, "no one else I've talked to has mentioned any of these things at all. We have been talking only about how X University can contribute to scientific and technical education around the world, and that's the thing that our president is really interested in. But what you say is very interesting, and I really want to think about it."

- In the winter of 2006 another prestigious U.S. university—let's call it Y—held a symposium celebrating a major anniversary, a centerpiece of which was to have been discussion of the future of liberal education.

A few months before the event, speakers who had agreed to be part of this were told that the focus had been changed and that they should just come and lecture to small departmental audiences on any topic they liked. A helpful and nicely talkative junior administrator told me that the reason for the change was that the president of Y had decided that a symposium on liberal education would not "make a splash," so he decided to replace it with one on the latest achievements in technology and their role in generating profits for business and industry.

There are hundreds of stories like these, and new ones arrive every day, in the United States, in Europe, in India, and, no doubt, in other parts of the world. We are pursuing the possessions that protect, please, and comfort us—what Tagore called our material "covering." But we seem to be forgetting about the soul, about what it is for thought to open out of the soul and connect person to world in a rich, subtle, and complicated manner; about what it is to approach another person as a soul, rather than as a mere useful instrument or an obstacle to one's own plans; about what it is to talk as someone who has a soul to someone else whom one sees as similarly deep and complex.

The word "soul" has religious connotations for many people, and I neither insist on these nor reject them. Each person may hear them or ignore them. What I do insist on, however, is what both Tagore and Alcott meant by this word: the faculties of thought and imagination that make us human and make our relationships rich human relationships, rather than relationships of mere use and manipulation. When we meet in society, if we have not learned to see both self and other in that way, imagining in one another inner faculties of thought and emotion, democracy is bound to fail, because democracy is built upon respect and concern, and these in turn are built upon the ability to see other people as human beings, not simply as objects.

Given that economic growth is so eagerly sought by all nations, especially at this time of crisis, too few questions have been posed about the direction of education, and, with it, of the world's democratic societies. With the rush to profitability in the global market, values precious for the future of democracy, especially in an era of religious and economic anxiety, are in danger of getting lost.

The profit motive suggests to many concerned leaders that science and technology are of crucial importance for the future health of their nations. We should have no objection to good scientific and technical education, and I shall not suggest that nations should stop trying to improve in this regard. My concern is that other abilities, equally crucial, are at risk of getting lost in the competitive flurry, abilities crucial to the health of any democracy internally, and to the creation of a decent world culture capable of constructively addressing the world's most pressing problems.

These abilities are associated with the humanities and the arts: the ability to think critically; the ability to transcend local loyalties and to approach world problems as a "citizen of the world"; and, finally, the ability to imagine sympathetically the predicament of another person.[2]

I shall make my argument by pursuing the contrast that my examples have already suggested: between an education for profit-making and an education for a more inclusive type of citizenship. I shall try to show how the humanities and arts are crucial both in primary/secondary and in university education, drawing examples from a range of different stages and levels. I do not at all deny that science and social science, particularly economics, are also crucial to the education of citizens. But nobody is suggesting leaving these studies behind. I focus, then, on what is both precious and profoundly endangered.

When practiced at their best, moreover, these other disciplines are infused by what we might call the spirit of the humanities: by searching critical thought, daring imagination, empathetic understanding of human experiences of many different kinds, and understanding of the complexity of the world we live in. Science education in recent years has rightly focused on educating the capacities for critical thinking, logical analysis, and imagining. Science, rightly pursued, is a friend of the humanities rather than their enemy. Although good science education is not my theme, a companion study on that topic would be a valuable complement to my focus on the humanities.[3]

The trends I deplore are worldwide, but I shall focus throughout on two very different nations that I know well: the United States, where I live and teach, and India, where my own global development work, much of it focused on education, has been conducted. India has a glorious tradition of humanities and arts education, exemplified in the theory and practice of the great Tagore, and I shall introduce you to his valuable ideas, which laid the foundations for a democratic nation and greatly influenced democratic education in Europe and the United States. But I shall also talk about the role of education in rural literacy projects for women and girls today, where the impetus to empower through the arts remains vital, and the effect of this empowerment on democracy can be clearly seen.

Where the United States is concerned, my argument will range over many types of educational experiments, from the use of Socratic self-examination in schools of many sorts to the role of arts organizations in plugging gaps in the public school curriculum. (The remarkable story of the Chicago Children's Choir in chapter will provide a detailed case study.)

Education does not take place only in schools. Most of the traits that are my focus need to be nurtured in the family as well, both in the early years and as children mature. Part of a comprehensive public policy approach to the questions this manifesto raises must include discussion of how families can be supported in the task of developing children's capabilities. The surrounding peer culture and the larger culture of social norms and political institutions also play an important role, either supporting or subverting the work done by schools and families. The focus on schools, colleges, and universities is justified, however, because it is in these institutions that the most pernicious changes have been taking place, as the pressure for economic growth leads to changes in curriculum, pedagogy, and funding. If we are aware that we are addressing just one part of the story of how citizens develop, we can pursue this focus without distortion.

Education is not just for citizenship. It prepares people for employment and, importantly, for meaningful lives. Another entire book could be written about the role of the arts and humanities in advancing these goals.[4] All modern democracies, however, are societies in which the meaning and ultimate goals of human life are topics of reasonable disagreement among citizens who hold many different religious and secular views, and these citizens will naturally differ about how far various types of humanistic education serve their own particular goals. What we can agree about is that young people all over the world, in any nation lucky enough to be democratic, need to grow up to be participants in a form of government in which the people inform themselves about crucial issues they will address as voters and, sometimes, as elected or appointed officials. Every modern democracy is also a society in which people differ greatly along many parameters, including religion, ethnicity, wealth and class, physical impairment, gender, and sexuality, and in which all voters are making choices that have a major impact on the lives of people who differ from themselves. One way of assessing any educational scheme is to ask how well it prepares young people for life in a form of social and political organization that has these features. Without support from suitably educated citizens, no democracy can remain stable.

I shall argue that cultivated capacities for critical thinking and reflection are crucial in keeping democracies alive and wide awake. The ability to think well about a wide range of cultures, groups, and nations in the context of a grasp of the global economy and of the history of many national and group interactions is crucial in order to enable democracies to deal responsibly with the problems we currently face as members of an interdependent world. And the ability to imagine the experience of another—a capacity almost all human beings possess in some form—needs to be greatly enhanced and refined if we are to have any hope of sustaining decent institutions across the many divisions that any modern society contains.

The national interest of any modern democracy requires a strong economy and a flourishing business culture. As I develop my primary argument, I shall also argue, secondarily, that this economic interest, too, requires us to draw on the humanities and arts, in order to promote a climate of responsible and watchful stewardship and a culture of creative innovation. Thus we are not forced to choose between a form of education that promotes profit and a form of education that promotes good citizenship. A flourishing economy requires the same skills that support citizenship, and thus the proponents of what I shall call "education for profit," or (to put it more comprehensively) "education for economic growth," have adopted an impoverished conception of what is required to meet their own

goal. This argument, however, ought to be subservient to the argument concerning the stability of democratic institutions, since a strong economy is a means to human ends, not an end in itself. Most of us would not choose to live in a prosperous nation that had ceased to be democratic. Moreover, although it is clear that a strong business culture requires some people who are imaginative and critical, it is that clear that it requires all people in a nation to gain these skills. Democratic participation makes wider demands, and it is these wider demands that my primary argument supports.

No system of education is doing a good job if its benefits reach only wealthy elites. The distribution of access to quality education is an urgent issue in all modern democracies. The Spellings Commission Report is to be commended for focusing on this question. It has long been a shameful feature of the United States, a wealthy nation, that access to quality primary/secondary education and especially access to college/university education is so unequally distributed. Many developing nations contain even larger disparities in access: India, for example, reports a male literacy rate of only around 65 percent, a female literacy rate of around 50 percent. Urban/rural disparities are larger. In secondary and higher education, there are even more striking gaps—between male and female, between rich and poor, between urban and rural. The lives of children who grow up knowing that they will go on to university and even postgraduate education are utterly different from the lives of children who in many cases do not get a chance to attend school at all. Much good work has been done on this question in many countries. It is not, however, the topic of this book.

This book is about what we should be striving for. Until we are clear about this, it is difficult to figure out how to get it to those who need it.

2 Music
Writing About Music and Dance

This chapter, "Writing About Music and Dance," discusses various types of writing about music and some different ways to write about musical works and musical performances. It includes examples of professional musicians and of non-musicians writing about music, including concerts. It concludes with a sample student research paper on a musical subject.

Music is not the easiest of the arts to write about. Part of the challenge of writing about music involves attempting to describe what the fleeting sounds are like. Confronted with this challenge, writers often resort to metaphor, particularly simile, to explain through the use of comparisons, what the music sounds like.

WRITING ABOUT MUSIC DIRECTLY

Among those who have written about music clearly and engagingly are the American composer Aaron Copland and the American composer, conductor, and teacher Leonard Bernstein.

Here, for example, is Leonard Bernstein describing a theme in the work of the Russian composer Peter Ilych Tchaikovsky:

> Let's just see how Tchaikovsky went about building up that lovely theme of his by simply repeating his ideas in a certain arranged order—what I like to call the 1-2-3 method. In fact so many famous themes are formed by exactly this method that I think you ought to know about it. Here's how it works: first of all there is a short idea, or phrase: (musical quote)—second, the same phrase is repeated, but with a small variation: (musical quote)—and third, the tune takes off in a flight of inspiration: (musical quote). 1, 2, and 3—like a 3-stage rocket, or like the countdown in a race: "On your mark, get set, go!" Or in target practice: "Ready, aim, fire!" Or in a movie studio: "Lights, camera, action!" It's always the same 1, 2, and 3!

11

Bernstein uses a series of similes, comparisons using "like," to explain how Tchaikovsky's theme contains three parts. The comparisons he makes are with things familiar to his audience—a group of children attending a lecture and concert.

Here is another example of a writer, this time the composer Aaron Copland, describing the musical element of timbre:

> After rhythm, melody, and harmony, comes timbre, or tone color. Just as it is impossible to hear speech without hearing some specific timbre, so can music exist only in terms of some specific color in tone. Timbre in music is analogous to color in painting. . . . Just as most mortals know the difference between white and green, so the recognition of differences in tone color is an innate sense with which most of us are born. It is difficult to imagine a person so "tone-blind" that he cannot tell a bass voice from a soprano, or, to put it instrumentally, a tuba from a cello.

Like Bernstein, Copland makes a comparison with something his audience understands, to help them understand something unfamiliar to them. Where Bernstein used simile, Copland develops an analogy, or extended comparison.

WRITING ABOUT MUSIC INDIRECTLY

In addition to writing about music directly as do Bernstein and Copland, writers sometimes write around the music, talking about music without actually describing what it sounds like. They might write about the life and times of a composer or performer; about the reasons for the rise and decline in popularity of a particular instrument or musical form or style; about a composer's or performer's influence, such as that of Beethoven or the Beatles.

Here, for example, is the American writer Ralph Ellison writing about the gospel singer Mahalia Jackson:

> There are certain women singers who possess, beyond all the boundaries of our admiration for their art, an uncanny power to evoke our love. We warm with pleasure at mere mention of their names; their simplest songs sing in our hearts like the remembered voices of old dear friends, and when we are lost within the listening anonymity of darkened concert halls, they seem to seek us out unerringly. Standing regal within the bright isolation of the stage, their subtlest effects seem meant for us and us alone; privately, as across the intimate space of our own living rooms. And when we encounter the simple dignity of their immediate presence, we suddenly ponder the mystery of human greatness.

Perhaps this power springs from their dedication, their having subjected themselves successfully to the demanding discipline necessary to the mastery of their chosen art. Or, perhaps, it is a quality with which they are born as some are born with bright orange hair. Perhaps, though we think not, it is acquired, a technique of "presence." But whatever its source, it touches us as a rich abundance of human warmth and sympathy. Indeed, we feel that if the idea of aristocracy is more than mere class conceit, then these surely are our natural queens. For they enchant the eye as they caress the ear, and in their presence we sense the full, moony glory of womanhood in all its mystery—maid, matron and matriarch. They are the sincere ones whose humanity dominates the artifices of the art with which they stir us, and when they sing we have some notion of our better selves.

Lotte Lehmann is one of these, and Marian Anderson. Both Madame Ernestine Schumann-Heink and Kathleen Ferrier possessed it. Nor is it limited to these mistresses of high art. Pastoria Pavon, "La Niña de Los Peines," the great flamenco singer, is another and so is Mahalia Jackson, the subject of this piece, who reminds us that while not all great singers possess this quality, those who do, no matter how obscure their origin, are soon claimed by the world as its own.

Reprinted from *Shadow and Act* (1995), by permission of Random House, Inc.

Ellison celebrates Jackson as a musician as well as a singer. He glories in how she sings and relishes the memory of hearing her in person. What makes Ellison's own memorializing of Mahalia Jackson memorable is the care he takes with his language, the precision of his vocabulary and the elegance and grace of his sentences. Look, for example, at the shape and listen to the sound of his first two sentences. This kind of concern with the how as well as the what—with style as well as with thought—makes for outstanding writing.

USING QUESTIONS TO WRITE ABOUT MUSIC

One way to approach writing about a musical subject is to frame one or more questions about it. You might ask, for example, "Why do people listen to music"? Or you might ask: "What kinds of effects does music have on people?" You might single out a particular type of music and create a question-topic, such as "How and Where did Rock (or Jazz) Originate?" Or: "What is the future of Rap (or Rock, or Classical) Music?"

In writing a research paper, you might trace the development of a performer's or composer's career. You could explore origins and influences, developments and continuities, changes and shifts of direction.

For such an assignment, you need to identify a composer or performer that interests you (or about whom you would like to learn more) and begin with some questions to guide your reading, listening, and research. Questions such as "Why did the Beatles become a musical phenomenon in the 1960s?" or "What was the Beatles' musical legacy?" or "What makes Chopin's musical career and musical style distinctive?" Once you have a good question, your research paper can become your way of answering it.

EXERCISES

1. Review a Music Concert
   Attend a concert of classical music. Take notes on the concert musical selections, the performers, the composers, the audience, the hall. Write a paper describing your experience of attending such a concert. Include your personal responses to the pieces on the program. You may also wish to do some library research about one or another of the works performed. And you may also use the concert program for information.

2. Interview and write about a city street and/or subway musicians. Find two or three street/subway musicians playing classical music—guitar, violin, cello—whatever you discover. Spend some time listening to each of them. Bring a notebook, and see if you can interview the performers about why they perform where they do, what kind of musical training they may have, what kinds of music they play, and why—and so on. Include your personal responses to the musicians and their music.

Following are additional questions you can use to direct your thinking when writing about music:

- What strikes you most forcibly about the music—and the lyrics, if there are any?
- What instruments are used—and how many of each?
- Who is the composer? When was the work composed?
- Where does it fit in the composer's career?
- Why was it composed—for what kind of occasion?
- What is its musical genre or type?
- What is the structure of the work? How is it organized?
- What style and period is the work written in? What features of the work—its melodies, harmonies, rhythms, structure—reflect the characteristics of the period (such as the classical era)?
- Which features of the work mark it as particularly reflective of the composer who wrote it?

- How would you characterize its musical language—medieval, Renaissance, baroque, romantic?
- What does the work express or convey? What feelings and ideas does it communicate?

Writing About a Musical Performance

One fairly common occasion for writing about music is reviewing a performance. Most major city newspapers review concerts—pop, jazz, and classical, including opera. Music critics for papers like the *Los Angeles Times* and the *Chicago Tribune* write regular review columns, usually with each reviewer specializing in a different type of music.

The following reviews, one of a rock concert and the other an opera performance, appeared in the *New York Times* on the same day. Read each review and answer the questions that follow them.

Voigt's Aida Is Assured
by
Anthony Tommasini

As opera fans everywhere know by now, Deborah Voigt's voice is gloriously suited to the German dramatic soprano repertory, especially Wagner and Strauss. But as she increasingly takes on weightier German roles, like Isolde, which she sings for the first time at the Vienna State Opera in May, she wants to keep the kind of lightness in her sound and smoothness in her legato that singing Italian repertory can provide. Though not an ideal match for Ms. Voigt's voice, the role of Verdi's Aida has been especially important to her.

Ms. Voigt sang her first "Aida" at the Met in 1999, a vocally tentative but honorable effort. In early 2001, she tried again. This time, though her singing was more confident, she seemed understandably rattled by her vocally and physically wobbly Radames, Luciano Pavarotti. Everyone in the cast and James Levine had to prop him up, sometimes literally. These turned out to be Mr. Pavarotti's last Met performances.

Ms. Voigt, strikingly slimmed down and exuding confidence, took over the title role of "Aida" on Thursday night in the Met's revival of its 1988 Sonja Frisell production. And this time, as Professor Higgins might say, "I think she's got it."

Sustained lyrical midrange singing and floated, high-lying Verdian phrases still did not come easily to her. You sensed

Ms. Voigt being careful to rein in her sound. But she never blustered her way through these passages, honored Verdi's dynamic markings and sang with genuine Italianate poignancy. Where impassioned, full-bodied singing was called for, Ms. Voigt filled the phrases with gleaming, dramatic soprano sound that lirico-spinto sopranos more suited to the role would covet. And as usual her musicianship was consistently impressive.

Ms. Voigt will sing two more performances of "Aida" on Tuesday and next Saturday.

Reprinted by permission from the *New York Times*, January 18, 2003.

Keith Richards Keeps the Stones Rolling
by
Ben Ratliff

Keith Richards is the formula for the Rolling Stones as well as its claim to spontaneity. The best moments of the Stones' show at Madison Square Garden on Thursday were introduced by his riffs, which appeared suddenly, bright, and cutting and emphasizing the weak beats of a rhythm. They sliced through the music's laggardly atmosphere.

When you're nearing 60, you don't cross through New York City four times on a yearlong world tour unless you have astounding amounts of money to make. (In September the band played at Madison Square Garden, Roseland Ballroom, and Giants Stadium; this "Forty Licks" tour will soon continue in Europe through August.)

A few years ago one witty reviewer wrote of one of the band's 1990's albums that it sounded as if the Stones had eliminated the in-between steps and recorded it inside a bank. But at some point in the 1970's, through its music and its publicity, the band really did create a kind of delicate golden mean, balancing rock, money, sloth, and sex; our culture has grown up understanding the proportions, and the context of popular culture prevents the group from seeming like venal laughingstocks.

Really, the Rolling Stones are predicated on good songwriting. The Stones rehearsed about 130 songs for this tour, and also revolved various sequences of songs that are deep-catalog although certainly not obscure. On Thursday at midconcert they played a triptych of songs from "Let It Bleed," flashing a giant image of the album's cover above them before and after the set.

An unsmiling Mick Jagger spent the show on his tiptoes, flopping from the elbows out and the knees down; he's still a great antivirtuosic dancer, if not the electrifying singer he was. The steady-enough rhythm section—the drummer Charlie Watts, the bassist Darryl Jones, and the keyboardist Chuck Leavell—hit some tempos that felt wrong (a too brisk "Angie," a mellow "Monkey Man") but also some that felt beautifully right, particularly a nasty, leisurely "Can't You Hear Me Knocking."

The same song pointed out the difference between the two guitarists, Ron Wood and Mr. Richards. Mr. Wood re-enacted the iconic solos recorded by Mick Taylor, his predecessor in the band; when casually improvising, he was a totally banal musician. Mr. Richards barely soloed, but when he did, each phrase had a spindly power and was based in rhythmic ideas. For long stretches, he parked in front of the drum set and locked into a groove.

The lasting image of the show, which was a run-through before another one to be broadcast live on HBO tonight, wasn't the red confetti during "Jumping Jack Flash." Nor was it the catwalk from a big stage to a small stage in the center of the arena—a device from the last tour—nor the thrashing return to the A section of "Midnight Rambler" after a five-minute slow-blues sojourn. It was Keith Richards, looking like a ragbag sponsored by Van Cleef & Arpels, sweetly smiling for the audience, and embracing his guitar: a startling, cuddly scene.

Reprinted by permission from the *New York Times*, January 18, 2003.

EXERCISE

Answer the following questions about the two reviews.

1. Which of the reviews engaged you the most? Why?
2. What similarities do you see in the opera and pop reviews?
3. How do each of the reviewers go about the business of actually describing the music?
4. How does each describe the performance?
5. What kinds of background and context does each reviewer provide?
6. What judgments does each reviewer render about the performance he attended?
7. Given the opportunity, would you be inclined to attend a performance by either of the artists reviewed here? Why or why not?

Sample Student Essay About Music

We conclude this chapter with an example of a student writing about music.

The author, Karen DiYanni, considers the significance of Richard Wagner's music, and the kind of influence the man and his music exerted on future generations of composers and musicians.

Notice how the author begins her paper with an epigraph, which suggests in a nutshell, the argument she will make in the paper overall. Notice, too, how she uses a comparison between Wagner's work and influence with that of Beethoven to clarify her ideas. And, notice, finally, how she introduces quotations and references from her sources.

The Importance of Richard Wagner

by

Karen DiYanni

"Of all the German figures of the nineteenth century, only Marx and Nietzsche had impacts equal to Wagner's on subsequent thought; like them, he could be attacked and parodied, but never ignored."

—Rey Longyear

Richard Wagner dominated the musical life of the second half of the nineteenth century as Beethoven dominated the musical world of the first half of the century (Schonberg 274). Both composers left their highly individual imprints on the music that would come after them. Both achieved greatness such that their works continue to serve as artistic monuments against which others' musical compositions are measured. Moreover, one might argue that Richard Wagner's operatic achievement compares with the achievement of Beethoven in symphonic music.

Unlike Beethoven, whose influence on future generations was confined to the realm of music, Richard Wagner's influence extended to art and politics. Also unlike Beethoven, whose works express a resilient optimism, a profound hope in human possibility, Wagner displays a more pessimistic attitude toward life. Influenced by the philosopher Arthur Schopenhauer, Wagner emphasizes the blind force of irrationality and passion that drive human behavior (Levy 251).

His operas portray characters whose lives are made unhappy by circumstances they cannot control, as in his most famous opera, *Tristan and Isolde*, in which the two lovers are kept apart only to be united in death.

Wagner was born in 1813, in the northern German city of Leipzig, home also to Bach and Handel, of Beethoven and Brahms. Unlike these musicians, all of whom were musically precocious, and all of whom received extensive musical instruction in their youth, Wagner, when young, was more interested in literature than in music. Shakespeare, in fact, was his idol (Schonberg 275). Wagner did not begin the serious study of music until age fifteen, and he never mastered a musical instrument as Bach and Handel mastered the organ and Beethoven and Brahms the piano. Wagner was also largely self-taught, mostly through intense study of the works of Beethoven (Schonberg 275). In fact, later in life, Wagner explained that he had wanted to do for opera what Beethoven had done for symphonic music—to make it express a wide range of experience, and to have it achieve overwhelming emotional effects. Wagner's admiration for Beethoven can be heard in the following comment from his writings:

> The last symphony of Beethoven is the redemption of music from out of her peculiar element into the realm of universal art. . . . for upon it the perfect art work of the future alone can follow (Schonberg 275).

Wagner believed that he and he alone could compose this "perfect art work of the future," and he believed that it could not be an orchestral work since Beethoven's mighty ninth symphony could never be surpassed. Instead, Wagner would create a new kind of opera, which he called "music drama" (Levy 251).

II

Wagnerian music drama attempted to bring together song and instrumental music, dance, drama and poetry in a single unbroken stream of art. Wagner did not like the way any of these arts had developed in his time. He thought that song in opera had been reduced to the operatic aria, that dance had become only ballet, and that music in opera had become reduced to a secondary role of accompanying the singers (Longyear 165). His ambitious goal was to restore the importance of music in opera, to establish a better balance between orchestra and singers. His goal also included raising the quality of the texts of operas. He attempted this in part by finding his subjects in medieval legend and Nordic mythology and partly by writing his own librettos (Longyear 166).

In honoring his musical forefather, Beethoven, Wagner would use the orchestra to do more than simply provide beautiful accompaniments for operatic arias. Instead Wagner's operatic orchestral writing would arouse intense emotion, "comment" on stage action, and be associated with incidents in the plot and characters' behavior. One important and influential way that Wagner accomplished these goals was by using what were called "leitmotifs" (Levy 252). These musical motives were usually brief fragments of melody or rhythm that, when played, would remind the audience of particular characters and actions, somewhat in the way a movie or television theme triggers associations in the mind of the audience.

III

From all accounts, Wagner was not a very nice human being. He was arrogant, willful, pompous, and rude. He was also a liar, a deadbeat, and a sensualist (Levy 250). He has been further described as "a selfish ingrate, an egotistical profligate, and an obnoxious megalomaniac" (Frost and McClure). And he was nothing if not ambitious. His ambition eventually paid off, for even after producing a number of failed operas, and after living in political exile in Switzerland for eleven years, he secured the patronage of King Ludwig II of Bavaria, who enabled Wagner to acquire wealth, fame, and power. Most important for Wagner was that with Ludwig's support, he could fulfill his dream of establishing an annual festival at which his (and only his) music dramas would be performed. Wagner designed the auditorium and the sets for productions of his monumental operatic works, some of them lasting for as long as six hours.

Wagner's works include the comic *Die Meistersinger*, the popular *Lohengrin* and the sensuous *Tristan and Isolde*, which influenced subsequent European musical style perhaps more than any work of the late nineteenth century. His tetralogy, *The Ring of the Niebelung*, which is generally considered his greatest work, includes four operas—*The Rhine Gold, The Valkyrie, Siegfried*, and *Twilight of the Gods*.

Because Wagner's music does not break easily into set pieces, it is difficult to illustrate his musical style. Complicating matters is that, like his great predecessor, Beethoven, his style developed and changed during his musical career, so much so that his music of the 1850s differs considerably from that of the 1870s (Schonberg 284). Nonetheless, something of the power Wagner could generate with an orchestra can be suggested with the Prelude to Act III of *Lohengrin*, especially in its opening and closing sections. The middle provides a brief hint of Wagner's lyrical style.

Alternatively, the mysterious quality of Wagner's music along with something of its relentless drive can be heard in his "Ride of the Valkyries" from his music drama *The Valkyrie*. Both of these excerpts provide examples of what might be called "Wagner's Greatest Hits." These popular selections, however, exist within a complex whole—the individual music dramas of which they are a part, and the entire range of Wagner's operatic output. As a result they can reflect only the slightest hint of his musical legacy. This legacy has been described best, perhaps, by the music historian Donald Grout, who sums up Wagner's enormous influence in this manner:

> Wagner's work affected all subsequent opera . . . His ideal of opera as a drama of significant content, with words, stage setting, visible action, and music all working in closest harmony toward the central purpose . . . was profoundly influential (Longyear 171).

IV

If Beethoven was the composer whose works crossed the bridge from the Classical style and outlook to a vision and style that is distinctively Romantic, Wagner is the composer whose greatest works epitomize that style and vision and bring it to its culmination. His music has long made such a powerful impression largely because of its "sheer overwhelming power" it creates in its listeners, "that all-embracing state of ecstasy, at once sensuous and mystical, toward which all Romantic art had been striving" (Grout and Palisca 752). He also served as the "father of modern music," introducing chromaticism and pointing to atonality with his masterpiece *Tristan and Isolde*.

Wagner's stature as one of music's all-time prominent composers is beyond question, as is his position as one of the nineteenth century's most influential and provocative individuals. His impact extended beyond music into politics and philosophy, and he has done much to shape the world we know today.

Works Cited

Frost, Thomas and John McClure. Liner notes for *The Wagner Album*. New York: Columbia Records, MG 30300, n.d.

Grout, Donald J. and Claude V. Palisca. *A History of Western Music*, 4th ed. New York: Norton, 1988.

Levy, Kenneth. *Music: A Listener's Introduction*. New York: Harper & Row, 1983.

Longyear, Rey M. *Nineteenth-Century Romanticism in Music*, 3rd ed. Englewood Cliffs, NJ: Prentice Hall, 1988.

Schonberg, Harold C. *The Lives of the Great Composers*, rev. ed. New York: Norton, 1981.

How Is It Put Together?

Understanding vocabulary and being able to identify its application in a musical work help us comprehend communication using the musical language, and thereby understand the creative communicative intent of the composer and the musicians who bring the composition to life. The ways in which musical artists shape the characteristics that follow bring us experiences that can challenge our intellects and excite our emotions. As in all communication, meaning depends on each of the parties involved; communicators and respondents must assume responsibility for facility in the language utilized.

Among the basic elements by which music is put together, we will identify and discuss seven: (1) Sound, (2) Rhythm, (3) Melody, (4) Harmony, (5) Tonality, (6) Texture, and (7) Musical Form.

SOUND

Music designs sound and silence. In the broadest sense, sound is anything that excites the auditory nerve: sirens, speech, crying babies, jet engines, falling trees, and so on. We might even call such sources noise. Musical composition, although it can even employ "noise," usually depends on controlled and shaped sound consistent in quality. We distinguish music from other sounds by recognizing four basic properties: (1) pitch, (2) dynamics, (3) tone color, and (4) duration.

Pitch

Pitch, the relative highness or lowness we hear in sound, represents a physical phenomenon measurable in vibrations per second. So, when we describe differences in pitch, we describe recognizable and measurable differences in sound waves. A pitch has a steady, constant frequency. A faster frequency produces a higher pitch; a slower frequency, a lower pitch. If we shorten a sounding body—a vibrating string, for example—it vibrates more rapidly. Musical instruments designed to produce high pitches, such as the piccolo, therefore tend to be small. Instruments designed to produce low pitches tend to be large—for instance, bass viols and tubas. In music, we call a sound that has a definite pitch a tone.

Color comprises a range of light waves within a visible spectrum. Sound also comprises a spectrum, one whose audible pitches range from 16 to 38,000 vibrations per second. We can perceive 11,000 different pitches, obviously more than practical for musical composition. Therefore, *by*

convention, musicians divide the sound spectrum into roughly ninety equally spaced frequencies comprising seven and a half *octaves.* The piano keyboard, consisting of eighty-eight keys (seven octaves plus two additional tones) representing the same number of equally spaced pitches, serves as an illustration (Fig. 4.1).

A scale, an arrangement of pitches or tones played in ascending or descending order, represents a conventional organization of the frequencies of the sound spectrum (Fig. 4.2). Not all music conforms to this convention. Music of Western civilization prior to approximately C.E. 1600 does not, nor does Eastern music, which makes great use of quarter tones. In addition, some contemporary Western music departs from the conventions of tonality of the major or minor scale. Islamic calls to prayer exhibit this quality. These examples represent cultures whose music does not conform to the Western conventions of pitch and scale, or tonality. Other characteristics, however, make this music sound different from the music of Bach, for example.

Dynamics

We call degrees of loudness or softness in music dynamics. Any tone can be loud, soft, or anywhere in between. Dynamics is the

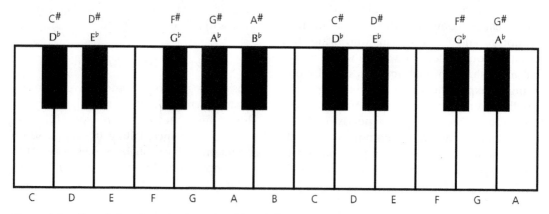

Figure 4.1 *Part of the piano keyboard and its pitches.*

A Question to Ask

Does this music sound like music typical of my culture? What musical characteristics make this so?

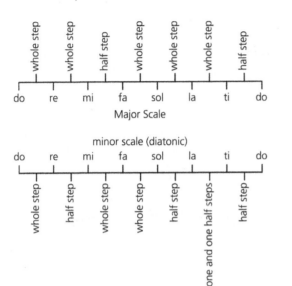

Figure 4.2 *The major and minor scales.*

decibel level of tones and depends on the physical phenomenon of *amplitude* of vibration. Greater force employed in the production of a tone results in wider sound waves and causes greater stimulation of the auditory nerves. The *size* of the sound wave, not its number of vibrations per second, changes.

Composers indicate *dynamic levels* with a series of specific notations:

pp	pianissimo (pee-yah-NEES—ee-moh)	very soft
p	piano	soft
mp	mezzo (MEHT-zoh) piano	moderately soft
mf	mezzo forte	moderately loud
f	forte (FOR-tay)	loud
ff	fortissimo (for-TEE-see-moh)	very loud

The notations of dynamics that apply to an individual tone, such as *p*, *mp*, and *f*, also may apply to a section of music. Changes in dynamics may be abrupt, gradual, wide, or small. A series of symbols also governs this aspect of music.

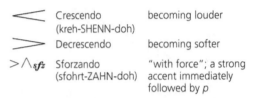

As we listen to and compare musical compositions, we can consider the use and breadth of dynamics in the same sense that we consider the use and breadth of palette in painting.

Tone Color

Tone color, or *timbre* (TAM-buhr), signifies the characteristic of tone that allows us to distinguish a pitch played on a violin, for example, from the same pitch played on a piano. In addition to identifying characteristic differences among sound-producing sources, tone color characterizes differences in quality of tones produced by the same source. Here the analogy of tone color is particularly appropriate. We call a tone produced with an excess of air—for example, by the human voice—"white." Figure 4.3 illustrates some of the various sources that produce musical tone and account for its variety of tone colors. The following table (Fig. 4.3) also lists these and other sources that produce musical tone and account for its timbres.

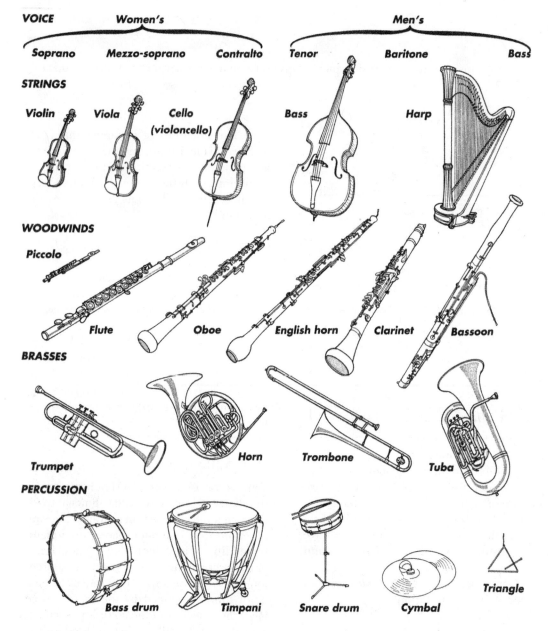

Figure 4.3   *The key sources of musical tone in an orchestra (instruments not to scale).*

Voice

Soprano	
Mezzo-soprano	} Women's
Contralto	
Tenor	
Baritone	} Men's
Bass	

Electronic

Synthesizer

Strings

Violin
Viola
Cello
(violoncello)
Bass
Harp

Woodwinds

Flute
Piccolo
Oboe
English horn
Clarinet
Bassoon

Brasses

Trumpet
Horn
Trombone
Tuba

Percussion

Snare drum   Piano   Harpsichord
Bass drum
Timpani
Triangle
Cymbal

The piano could be considered either a stringed or a percussion instrument because it produces its sound by vibrating strings *struck* by hammers. The harpsichord's strings are set in motion by plucking.

Electronically produced music, available since the development of the RCA synthesizer at the Columbia-Princeton Electronics Music Center, has become a standard source in assisting contemporary composers (Fig. 4.4). Originally electronic music fell into two categories: (1) the electronic altering of acoustically produced sounds, which came to be labeled as *musique concrète* (see Glossary), and (2) electronically generated sounds. However, advances in technology have blurred those differences over the years.

Figure 4.4 *Musician at an electronic control panel. Randy Matusow/Monkmeyer Press.*
Source: Cameramann/The Image Works.

Synthesizing technology took an important step forward with the development of MIDI (pronounced mih-dee; for musical instrument digital interface), a standard adopted by manufacturers for interfacing synthesizer equipment. MIDI allowed the device played on to be separated from tone production; for example, keyboards that look, feel, and play like a piano and string controllers that play like a violin. In addition, control signals can be fed to and from a MIDI instrument into and out of a personal computer so users can edit and store music and convert to and from musical notation. Computers now can act as controllers to drive MIDI equipment and used for direct digital synthesis.

Duration

Duration, another characteristic of sound, constitutes the length of time in which vibration is maintained without interruption. Duration in musical composition uses a set of conventions called musical notation (Fig. 4.5). This system consists of a series of symbols (notes) by which the composer indicates the relative duration of each tone. The system is progressive—that is, each note is either double or half the duration of an adjacent note. Musical notation also includes a series of symbols that denote the duration of *silences* in a composition. These symbols, called *rests*, have the same durational values as the symbols for duration of tone.

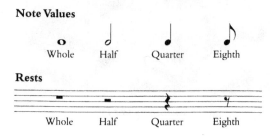

Figure 4.5 *Musical notation.*

RHYTHM

Rhythm comprises recurring pulses and accents that create identifiable patterns. Without rhythm we have only an aimless rising and falling of tones. Earlier we noted that each tone and silence has duration. Composing music means placing each tone into a time or rhythmical relationship with every other tone. As with the dots and dashes of the Morse code, we can "play" the rhythm of a musical composition without reference to its tones. Each symbol (or note) of the musical notation system denotes a duration relative to every other symbol in the system. Rhythm consists of: (1) beat, (2) meter, and (3) tempo.

Beat

The individual pulses we hear are called beats. Beats may be grouped into rhythmic patterns by placing accents every few beats. Beats represent basic units of time and form the background against which the composer places notes of various lengths.

Meter

Normal musical practice groups clusters of beats into units called *measures*. When these groupings are regular and reasonably equal they comprise *simple* meters. When the number of beats in a measure equals three or two it constitutes *triple* or *duple* (DOO-puhl) meter. As listeners, we can distinguish between duple and triple meters because of their different *accent* patterns. In triple meter we hear an accent every third beat—ONE two three, ONE two three—and in duple meter the accent is every other beat—ONE two, ONE two. If there are four beats in a measure, the second accent is weaker than the first— ONE two THREE four, ONE two THREE four. When accent occurs on normally unaccented beats, we have *syncopation*.

Tempo

Tempo is the rate of speed of the composition. A composer may notate tempo in two ways. The first involves a *metronome marking*, such as ♩= 60. This means playing or singing the piece at the rate of sixty quarter notes (♩) per minute. The other method, although less precise, involves more descriptive terminology in Italian.

The tempo may be quickened or slowed, and the composer indicates this by the words *accelerando* (accelerate) and *ritardando* (retard, slow down). A performer who takes liberties with the tempo uses *rubato* (roo-BAH-toh).

Largo (broad) Grave (grahv) (grave, solemn)	Very slow
Lento (slow) Adagio (ah-DAHZH-ee-oh) (leisurely)	Slow
Andante (at a walking pace) Andantino (somewhat faster than andante) Moderato (moderate)	Moderate
Allegretto (briskly) Allegro (cheerful, faster than allegretto)	Fast
Vivace (vih-VAH-chay) (vivacious) Presto (very quick) Prestissimo (as fast as possible)	Very fast

MELODY

Melody is a succession of sounds with rhythmic and tonal organization. We can visualize melody as linear and essentially horizontal. Thus, any organization of musical tones occurring *one after another* constitutes a melody. Two other terms, *tune* and *theme*, relate to melody as parts to a whole. For example, the *tune* in Figure 4.6 is a melody—that is, a succession of tones. However, a melody is not always a tune. In general, the term *tune* implies singability, and many melodies cannot be sung. A *theme* is also a melody. However, in musical composition, it specifically means a central musical idea, which may be restated and varied throughout a piece. Thus, a melody is not necessarily a theme.

Related to theme and melody, the *motif* (moh-TEEF), or *motive*, constitutes a short melodic or rhythmic idea around which a composer may design a composition. For example, in Beethoven's Symphony No. 5 in C minor, the first movement develops around a motif of four notes.

In listening for how a composer develops melody, theme, and motive, we can use two terms to describe what we hear: *conjunct* and *disjunct*. Conjunct melodies comprise notes close together, stepwise, on the musical scale. For example, the interval between the opening notes of the soprano line of J. S. Bach's (1685–1750) chorale "Jesu Joy of Man's Desiring" from his Cantata 147 (Fig. 4.7) never occupy more than a whole step. Such melodic development is highly conjunct. Disjunct melodies contain intervals of a third or more. However, no formula determines disjunct or conjunct characteristics; no line exists at which a melody ceases to be disjunct and becomes conjunct. These constitute relative and comparative terms that assist us in description. For example, we would say that the opening melody of "The Star Spangled Banner" (Fig. 4.6) is more disjunct than the opening melody of "Jesu Joy of Man's Desiring"—or that the latter is more conjunct than the former.

Figure 4.6 *"The Star Spangled Banner" (excerpt).*

Je - su joy of man's de - sir - ing

Figure 4.7   *"Jesu Joy of Man's Desiring" (excerpt).*

HARMONY

When two or more tones sound at the same time, we have harmony. Harmony is essentially a vertical arrangement, in contrast with the horizontal arrangement of melody.

However, as we shall see, harmony also has a horizontal property—movement forward in time. In listening for harmony, we are interested in how simultaneous tones *sound together.*

Two tones played simultaneously are an *interval;* three or more form a *chord.* When we hear an interval or a chord, we first respond to its *consonance* or *dissonance.* Consonant harmonies sound stable in their arrangement. Dissonant harmonies sound tense and unstable. Consonance and dissonance, however, are not absolute properties. Essentially they are conventional and, to a large extent, cultural. What sounds dissonant to our ears may not to someone else's. In musical response, we must determine *how* the composer utilizes these two properties. Most Western music is primarily consonant. Dissonance, on the other hand, can be used for contrast, to draw attention to itself, or as a normal part of *harmonic progression.*

As its name implies, harmonic progression involves the movement forward in time of harmonies. In discussing pitch, we noted the convention of the major and minor scales—that is, the arrangement of the chromatic scale into a system of *tonality.* When we play or sing a major or minor scale, we note a particular phenomenon: Our movement from *do* to *re* to *mi* to *fa* to *sol* to *la* seems smoothly natural. But when we reach the seventh tone of the scale, *ti,* something strange happens. It seems as though we must continue back to *do,* the *tonic* of the scale. Sing a major scale and stop at *ti.* You feel uncomfortable. Your mind tells you to *resolve* that discomfort by returning to *do.* That same sense of tonality—that sense of the tonic—applies to harmony. Within any scale, a series of chords may be developed on the basis of the individual tones of the scale. Each of the chords has a subtle relationship to each of the other chords and to the tonic—that is, the *do* of the scale. That relationship creates a sense of progression that leads back to the chord based on the tonic (note the basic chordal progression of rock and roll—I–IV–V–I—discussed earlier in the chapter).

We call the harmonic movement toward, and either resolving or not resolving to, the tonic, *cadence* (Fig. 4.8). Composers use cadence as one way of articulating sections of a composition or of surprising us by upsetting our expectations. A composer using a full cadence uses a harmonic progression that resolves just as our ear tells us it should. We have a sense of ending, of

Figure 4.8   *Full cadence in the key of C.*

completeness. However, when a composer uses a half cadence or a deceptive cadence, she upsets the expected progression, and the musical development moves in an unexpected direction.

As we listen to music of various historical periods, we may note that in some compositions tonal centers are blurred because composers frequently *modulate*—that is, change from one key (see Glossary) to another. In the twentieth century, many composers (see Serialism, p. 139), some of them using purely mathematical formulas to utilize equally all tones of the chromatic scale, have removed tonality as an arranging factor and have developed *atonal* music, or music without tonality. A convention of harmonic progression is disturbed when tonality is removed. Nonetheless, we still have harmonic progression, and we still have harmony—dissonant or consonant.

TONALITY

Utilization of tonality, or key, has taken composers in various directions over the centuries. Conventional tonality, employing the major and minor scales and keys we discussed previously relative to pitch, forms the basis for most sixteenth- to twentieth-century music, as well as traditionally oriented music of the twentieth century. In the early twentieth century, traditional tonality was abandoned by some composers, and a new *atonal* harmonic expression occurred. Atonal compositions seek the freedom to use any combination of tones without the necessity of having to resolve chordal progressions.

TEXTURE

The term *texture* has various spatial connotations. Texture in painting and sculpture denotes surface quality: roughness or smoothness. Texture in weaving denotes the interrelationship of the warp and the woof (the horizontal and vertical threads in fabric). In music, texture has three characteristics: monophony, polyphony, and homophony.

Monophony

When we have a single musical line without accompaniment, we have a texture called monophonic. Many voices or instruments may be playing at the same time, but as long as they sing the same notes at the same time—in unison—the texture remains monophonic. G.F. Handel's (1685–1759) "Hallelujah" Chorus has instances in which men and women sing the same notes in different octaves. This still represents monophony.

Polyphony

Polyphony or counterpoint means "many-sounding," and it occurs when two or more melodic lines of relatively equal interest are performed at the same time. We can hear it in a very simple statement in Josquin Desprez's (day-PRAY; 1440–1521) "Ave Maria . . . Virgo Serena." Palestrina's "Kyrie" from the *Pope Marcellus Mass* has more complexity. When the counterpoint uses an immediate restatement of the musical idea, then the composer employs *imitation*.

Homophony

When chords accompany one main melody, we have homophonic texture. Here the composer focuses attention on the melody by supporting it with subordinate sounds.

Of course, composers may change textures within a piece, as Handel does in the "Hallelujah" Chorus. This creates an even richer fabric of sound for our response.

A Question of Style

Serialism

serialism (SIHR-ee-uh-lihz-uhm). In music, a mid-twentieth-century type of composition based on the twelve-tone system. In serialism, the techniques of the twelve-tone system are used to organize musical dimensions other than pitch, for example, rhythm, dynamics, and tone color. At the root of the movement was Arnold Schoenberg (SHURN-bairk; 1874–1951). Between 1905 and 1912 Schoenberg moved away from the gigantic post-Romantic works he had been composing and began to adopt a more contained style, writing works for smaller ensembles, and treating instruments in a more individual manner. Although the word *atonality*, meaning without tonality, describes Schoenberg's works, he preferred the term *pantonality*—inclusive of all tonalities. In his compositions, Schoenberg used any combination of tones without having to resolve chord progressions, a concept he called "the emancipation of dissonance." He broke down the musical texture, alternating timbres swiftly and fragmenting rhythm and melody. In 1911, Schoenberg wrote *Six Little Piano Pieces, op. 19.* In these, he made some advances in his new style and eliminated some of the traditional procedures, for example, repetition or recall of earlier musical statements. These short pieces contain only nine to eighteen measures. Nonetheless, each, like "Etwas rasch" (rather quick), constitutes a tiny but freestanding presentation of expression.

MUSICAL FORM

Tones and rhythms that proceed without purpose or stop arbitrarily make little sense to the listener. Therefore, just as the painter, sculptor, or any other artist must try to develop design that has focus and meaning, the musician must attempt to create a coherent composition of sounds and silences. The principal means by which artists create coherence is repetition. Music achieves coherence, or unity, through repetition in a similar fashion. However, because music deals with time as opposed to space, repetition in music usually involves recognizable themes.

Thus, we can define form as organization through repetition to create unity.

Binary form, as the name implies, consists of two parts: the opening section of the composition and a second part that often acts as an answer to the first: AB. Each section is then repeated.

A Question to Ask

What kind or kinds of texture appear in this composition?

Ternary form is a three-part development in which the opening section repeats after the development of a different second section: ABA.

Ritornello (rih-tor-NEHL-loh), which developed in the baroque period, and *rondo*, which developed in the classical period, employ a continuous development that returns to modified versions of the opening theme after separate treatments of additional themes. Ritornello alternates orchestral or *ripieno* passages with solo passages. Rondo alternates a main theme in the tonic key with subordinate themes in contrasting keys.

Sonata form, or *sonata–allegro form* takes its name from the conventional treatment of the first movement of the sonata. It also serves as the form of development of the first movement of many symphonies: ABA or AABA. The first A section, known as the *exposition*, states two or three main and subordinate themes. To cement the perception of section A, the composer may repeat it: AA. The B section, the *development*, takes the original themes and develops them with several fragmentations and modulations. The movement then returns to the A section: This final section, called the *recapitulation*, usually does not exactly repeat the opening section; in fact, it may be difficult to recognize in some pieces. In Mozart's Symphony No. 40, the opening movement (allegro) employs sonata–allegro form. However, we recognize the recapitulation section only by a very brief restatement of the first theme, as heard in the exposition, and not as a repetition of the opening section. Then, after a lengthy *bridge*, the second theme from the exposition appears. Mozart closes the movement with a brief *coda*, or closing section, in the original key, based on the first phrase of the first theme.

The *fugue*, which we introduced earlier, is a polyphonic development of one, two, or sometimes three short themes. Fugal form, which takes its name from the Latin *fuga* ("flight"), has a traditional, although not a necessary, scheme of development with two common characteristics: (1) counterpoint and (2) a clear dominant-tonic relationship—that is, imitation of the theme at the fifth above or below the tonic. Each voice in a fugue (as many as five or more) develops the basic subject independent from the other voices, and passes through as many of the basic elements as the composer deems necessary. Unification results not by a return to an opening section, as in closed form, but by the varying recurrences of the subject throughout.

The *canon*, a contrapuntal form based on note-for-note imitation of one voice by another, separates the voices by a brief time interval—for example (the use of letters here does not indicate sectional development):

Voice 1: a b c d e f g
Voice 2:   a b c d e f g
Voice 3:   a b c d e f g

The interval of separation can vary among the voices. The canon differs from the *round*, for example "Row, row, row your boat." A round is also an exact melodic repeat. The canon develops new material indefinitely: The round repeats the same phrases over and over. The interval of separation in the round stays constant—a phrase apart.

Variation form modifies an initial theme through melodic, rhythmic, and harmonic treatments, each more elaborate than the last. Each section usually ends with a strong cadence, and the piece ends, literally, when the composer decides he or she has done enough.

Questions to Consider

To begin the process of musical analysis, one should consider several basic questions. Is this particular work organized as a coherent unit? If so, what is the basis of its coherence? What makes this work a unified whole? Is it based on one of the traditional structural patterns, such as sonata-allegro, minuet and trio, or theme and variations, or does it have some other form? We can always assume that musical works are based on some principle of organization, standard or not; unless at some level we sense some logic and coherence in a work, we dismiss it as random, inartistic, and a waste of our time and attention. Identifying the musical means by which the composer has built in unity and coherence is a fundamental step in analysis.

Another basic question in stylistic analysis is how a particular work relates to the stylistic developments of its time. Is it a venture into completely new territory, or does it build on established styles? Is it a further refinement of a style in which the composer has worked previously, or is the composer experimenting with new stylistic ideas? In what way has the composer worked out his own individual version of an established style? For example, when Stravinsky and Copland venture into twelve-tone writing, do they create unique, personal versions of the style? Can you still hear their personal style in these works, or do their twelve-tone works sound just like other composers' twelve-tone works?

A related issue is the question of whether the composer was influenced by another composer. Sometimes the line of influence is obvious: We know that the shadow of Beethoven inspired Brahms but also daunted him; he hesitated for years before allowing his First Symphony to be performed, knowing that it would be compared to the symphonies of Beethoven. On the other hand, claims of another composer's influence are sometimes difficult to support. Similarity of style is not enough in itself to justify such a claim, since there are several other possible explanations for such similarity. The line of influence might run in the opposite direction, or both might have been influenced by a third composer or a pervasive style of the period. It is difficult to prove influence from the music alone, unless we have the composer's own words or some other historical evidence that establishes a connection. Within these limits, however, the question of influence and the other general questions listed earlier can be helpful ways to approach the crucial issue of where a work fits in the overall history of a style.

Another possible direction to pursue when beginning an analysis project is relating a particular work to the surrounding culture and contemporary developments in the other arts. At some times in history, the connections between music and the other arts are particularly obvious. French art songs of the late nineteenth and early twentieth centuries, for example, cannot be understood without reference to the symbolist literary movement, the source of the evocative texts that attracted composers, determined their musical choices, and led them to create a new musical style. Likewise, the songs of Schoenberg and Berg cannot be understood without some understanding of the expressionist movement in German art and literature. We often use terms borrowed from the world of the literary and visual arts, such as impressionism and expressionism, to describe musical styles; we cannot discuss impressionism or expressionism in music without first understanding what the terms mean in their original context. In addition, it is obvious that programmatic music cannot be analyzed without some reference to the story or picture the music depicts.

The question of cultural context affects all music, not just those musical styles obviously influenced by the visual or literary arts. The physical setting in which music was performed, the audience for whom it was intended, the context that called for a performance, and the way a particular society viewed the roles of composer and performer—all these issues have an influence on issues of style. Understanding a musical work may involve research into these broader questions. We need to be aware of musical life in earlier ages, the performing forces composers had at their disposal, and the context in which music was performed. In order to understand the cantatas of Bach, for example, we must understand that they were not created to be concert pieces; they were intended to be performed in a small church as part of a four-hour Sunday service. In addition, we cannot understand this music without some sense of the religious movement known as Pietism and its effect on religious ideas and approaches to worship in the Lutheran Church of Bach's day. The better we understand the original purpose of a musical work, the audience for whom it was intended, and the circumstances of its first performance, the better prepared we are to make sense of the music.

Another fundamental question to raise in the early stages of an analysis project is the composer's intent. Composers write music for many different reasons, and understanding their motivation may very well be the key to understanding the music they produce.

Sometimes when a composer writes music for a particular occasion, that special purpose determines the style of the music. A famous example of music for a special occasion is "Nuper rosarum flores," a motet by Guillaume Dufay, one of the masterpieces of the early Renaissance. The piece is remarkably complex. Not only does it utilize the fourteenth-century compositional process of isorhythm; it further complicates the process by utilizing two isorhythmic tenors that move in canon at the fifth. Further, the large sections of the piece are organized in different rhythmic proportions—another process used by earlier composers, but utilized here in a more complicated way. Of course one could analyze the motet from the score alone, but it makes more sense to see the work in its historical context. The motet was commissioned in 1436 for the dedication of Brunelleschi's new dome for the cathedral in Florence. This ceremony was an important occasion in Renaissance Italy; the Pope was in attendance, and the fact that Dufay was asked to write special music for this ceremony was a sign of the high regard in which he was held. Recent scholarship has made a convincing argument that the double-tenor structure of Dufay's piece was intended to mirror in music the mathematical elements of Brunelleschi's bold design for the large unsupported dome. The proportions of the sections may also have been based on the proportions of the finished basilica or the proportions of Solomon's Temple as described in the Bible. In other words, the circumstances explain the complex structure of the music, and it would be a mistake to treat this piece as if it were an ordinary motet.

Composers have often written music for particular performers, and that circumstance should help us understand those works. Compositional choices may be based on the particular talents of the performers for whom the works are intended, and the question of expanded instrumental idiom may be a central question to raise in the analytical process.

Sometimes the composer's main purpose is to experiment with new materials or structures. In much of the modernist music composed in the second half of the twentieth century, composers are intent on creating new styles, sometimes with each new work. George Crumb, for example, often combines in his music ideas borrowed from Eastern music, astronomy, ritual, and drama, and one should take these ideas into account in approaching his works. If a composer has organized a particular work around mathematical structures, has ordered all the elements serially, or has integrated musical ideas from other cultures into Western structures, we cannot analyze or appreciate the work except in those terms.

Sometimes, on the other hand, a composer may be refining an established style, and one must view the work against the background of that established style. That is the case with much of the music from the standard-practice period. When we approach a Mozart symphony, we know how to proceed, armed with our understanding of the principles of classical structure. When a composer moves from one style to another, as Stravinsky did in his later years, we have to be aware of that change; it would make no sense to analyze his serial works using the same criteria we would use to analyze his neoclassical works.

Finally, if a composer has written a programmatic work, we must judge the music in those terms; we cannot adequately appreciate the music without some understanding of the program. The same holds true for text setting in song and opera; the complex relationship between text and music is one of the major questions to consider in the process of analysis.

In short, we should judge musical works against the background of what the composer was trying to do. To ignore available information about the composer's intent is to deprive ourselves of useful information about the directions the analysis should take. In some cases, we may have to begin our analysis by study of the composer's ideas and aims, so that we can approach the music as he or she approached it and use criteria that are appropriate for this specific work.

Visual Art

ART AND THE ARTIST

What is art? Few questions have given rise to so many different answers. The problem, as we see in the above cartoon, is that art is an object and a word. Both vary widely in different times and places and in different cultures. In the past hundred years they have changed so much that all the old definitions and even the categories of art are obsolete. The reason is not hard to find: more change occurred in the twentieth century than in any other period in history. The modern era has been both exhilarating and disturbing. It opened up new horizons that greatly expanded life's possibilities, but at the same time it challenged our most cherished beliefs. Art as we know it is a direct outgrowth of the industrialized world, with its advanced technology, global economy, large middle-class yet highly fragmented society, and democratic institutions. Under such unique conditions it is impossible to come up with a universally valid definition of art. We must therefore leave this task to philosophers and aestheticians.

Nevertheless, there is still a good deal that can be said. Looking again at our cartoon, we see that art is not just any kind of object. It is an aesthetic object. Art is meant to be looked at and appreciated for its own sake. Its special qualities set art apart, so that it is often placed away from everyday life—in museums, caves, or churches—though much of it was made to be lived with. What does aesthetic mean? It is defined as "that which concerns the beautiful." Of course, not all art is beautiful to each person's eyes, but it is still art. No matter how unsatisfactory, the term will have to do for lack of a better one.

Aesthetics is a branch of philosophy that has occupied thinkers from Plato to the present day. Like all philosophical matters, it is subject to debate. During the last hundred years, aesthetics has also become a field of psychology, which has come to equally little agreement. Why is this so? On the one hand, people the world over make many of the same basic judgments. Our brains and nervous systems are the same because, according to recent theory, every human being is descended from one woman who lived in Africa a quarter-million years ago. On the other hand, taste is a product of culture, which is so varied that it is impossible to judge art by any one set of standards. It seems, therefore, that we cannot establish absolute standards for judging art. Instead, we must view works of art in the context of the culture in which they were created, whether past or present. How indeed could it be otherwise, so long as art is still being created all around us, opening our eyes almost daily to new experiences and forcing us to adjust our thinking?

Imagination

We all dream. That is imagination at work. To imagine means to make an image— a picture—in our minds. Human beings are not the only creatures who have imagination. Animals also dream. However, humans are the only creatures who can tell one another about imagination in words, pictures, or music. No other animal has ever been observed to draw a recognizable image spontaneously in the wild. In fact, their only images have been produced under carefully controlled laboratory conditions that tell us more about the experiment than they do about art. There can be little doubt, though, that humans have the ability to create art. By the age of five every normal child has drawn a moon pie-face. This ability is one of our most distinctive features.

Imagination is a mysterious gift. It can be viewed as the link between the conscious and the subconscious, where most of our brain activity takes place. it is the glue that holds our personality, intellect, and spirituality together. Because it responds to all three, it acts in ways that are determined by the mind. Imagination is important, as it allows us to conceive of all kinds of possibilities in the future and to understand the past in a way that has real survival value. It therefore is an essential part of our makeup. In contrast, the ability to make art must have been acquired relatively recently in the course of human evolution. Human beings have been walking the earth for nearly 4.5 million years, although our own species (home sapiens) is much younger than that. By comparison, the oldest known prehistoric art was made only about 35,000 years ago, but it was undoubtedly the culmination of long process of development that we cannot trace because the record of the earliest art is lost.

Who were the first artists? In all likelihood, they were shamans. Like the legendary Greek poet Orpheus, who sang his words while playing the lyre, they were believed to have divine powers of inspiration and to be able to enter the underworld of the subconscious in a deathlike trance—but unlike ordinary mortals, they could then return to the realm of the living. With this unique ability to penetrate the unknown and express it through art, the artist-shaman gained control over the forces hidden in human beings and nature. Even today artists are magicians whose work can mystify and move us—an embarrassing fact to civilized people, who do not like to give up their veneer of rational control.

Creativity

The making of a work of art is much like the story of Creation told in the Bible. However, this divine ability was not fully realized until Michelangelo described the creative experience as "liberating the figure from the marble that imprisons it." Perhaps that is why the concept of creativity was once reserved for God, as only he could give material form to an idea. In human terms, the metaphor of birth comes closer to the truth than the notion of a transfer or projection of an image from the artist's mind. The making of a work of art is both joyous and painful, full of surprises, and in no sense mechanical. Moreover, artists themselves tend to look upon their creations as living things. This magical aspect of art was given charming expression by the Roman poet Ovid in his *Metamorphoses*. He tells the story of Pygmalion, who carved such a beautiful statue of the nymph Galatea that he fell in love with it and prayed to Venus, the goddess of love, to bring it to life. Fortunately for him, his wish was granted. (The tale is familiar to us as the basis for the musical *My Fair Lady*.) We can readily understand the tale when it comes to realistic sculpture. But would the artist feel the same way today, when abstract art is the norm? Strange though it may seem, the answer is Yes, as the cartoon on this page suggests. The reason is that a work represents the artist's highest aspirations and deepest understanding, no matter what form it takes.

The creation of a work of art has little in common with what we usually mean by making. It is a strange and risky business in which the makers never quite know what they are making until they have actually made it. To put it another way, making art is like a game of hide-and-seek in which the seekers are not sure what they are looking for until they have found it. In some cases, it is the bold "finding" that impresses us most; in others, it is the strenuous "seeking." For the non-artist, it is hard to believe that this uncertainty, this need to take a chance, is the essence of the artist's work. Whereas artisans generally attempt what they know to be possible, artists are driven to attempt the impossible—or at least the improbable or seemingly unimaginable. What defines art, then, is not any difference in materials or techniques from the applied arts. Rather, art is defined by the artist's willingness to take risks in the quest for bold, new ideas.

What sets great artists apart from others is not simply the desire to seek but the mysterious ability to find. This talent is often called a "gift," implying that it is a sort of present from some higher power. It is also described as "genius," a term that originally meant that a higher power—kind of "good demon"—inhabits and acts through the artist. When creativity is at its height, artists speak of being inspired by the muses that were believed to govern the liberal arts in antiquity. And when the well runs dry, they feel as if the muse has abandoned them.

Inspiration is sometimes experienced as a sudden leap of the imagination, but only rarely does a new idea emerge full-blown like the Greek goddess Athena from the head of Zeus, her father. Instead, it is usually preceded by a long period in which all the hard work is done without finding the solution to the problem. At the critical point, the imagination makes connections between seemingly unrelated parts. Ordinarily, artists work with materials that have little or no shape of their own. The creative process then consists of a long series of smaller leaps of the imagination and the artist's attempts to give them form by shaping the material.

One of the attributes that distinguishes great artists is their great mastery of technique, which enables them to give their ideas full expression in visible form. Their superior ability is recognized by other artists, who admire their work and seek to emulate it. This is not to say that facility alone is all that is needed. Far from it! The academic painters and sculptors of the nineteenth century were among the most proficient artists in history—as well as the dullest. Clearly, the making of a work of art should not be confused with manual skill or craftsmanship. Some works of art may demand a great deal of technical skill; others do not. And even the most painstaking piece of craft does not deserve to be called a work of art unless it involves a leap of the imagination.

Nor should talent be confused with aptitude. Aptitude is what the artisan needs. It means a better-than-average knack for doing something. An aptitude is fairly constant and specific. It can be measured with some success by means of tests that permit us to predict future performance. Creative talent, on the other hand, is utterly unpredictable. It can be spotted only on the basis of past performance. Even past performance is not enough to ensure that a given artist will continue to produce on the same level. Some artists reach a creative peak early in their careers and then "go dry," while others,

after a slow start, may do astonishingly original work in middle age or even later.

Originality and Tradition

Originality is what distinguishes art from craft. It is the yardstick of artistic greatness or importance. Unfortunately, it is also very hard to define. The usual synonyms—uniqueness, novelty, freshness—do not help us very much. Unless a work is a copy, the problem comes not in deciding whether it is original but in saying exactly how original it is. In addition, every work of art has its own place in tradition. Without tradition—the word means "that which has been handed down to us"—no originality would be possible. Tradition provides the platform from which artists make their leap of the imagination. The place where they land becomes the point of departure for further leaps. Tradition also serves as the meeting ground of art and craft. What the art student or apprentice learns are skills and techniques: ways of drawing, painting, carving, designing—established ways of seeing.

For us, too, tradition is essential. Whether we are aware of it or not, tradition is the framework within which we form our opinions of works of art and assess their originality. This is especially true of masterpieces, the standards by which we measure other works of art. A masterpiece is a work that can bear close scrutiny and withstand the test of time. Such judgments are always subject to revision, however. In fact, tastes have varied greatly over time. Works that were once thought of as cornerstones of tradition have been discarded, while others that were ignored or even despised are now seen as important. Thus the "canon," or core body, of Western art is not static and unchanging but is constantly shifting. Although it is fashionable to attack the idea of a canon, some works really are better than others, whether we wish to acknowledge it or not.

Meaning and Style

Why do people create art? Surely one reason is the urge to adorn themselves and decorate the world around them. Both are part of a larger desire, not merely to remake the world in their image but to recast themselves and their environment in ideal form. Art is, however, much more than decoration. Like science and religion, it fulfills the urge of human beings to understand themselves and the universe. This function makes art especially important and worthy of our attention. Art allows us to communicate our understanding in ways that cannot be expressed otherwise. In art, as in language, people invent symbols that convey complex thoughts in new ways. We must think of art not in terms of prose but of poetry, which is free to rearrange words and syntax in order to convey new, often multiple, meanings and moods. A work of art likewise suggests much more than it states. And as with poetry, the value of art lies equally in what it says and how it says it. But what is art trying to say? Artists often provide no clear explanation, since the work itself is the statement. If they could say what they mean in words, they would be writers instead.

Nevertheless, art is full of meaning, even if its content is slender or obscure at times. What do we mean by content? The word refers not only to a work's subject and literal meaning (its iconography) but to its appearance as well, for the visual elements are themselves filled with significance. Hence the content of art is inseparable from its formal qualities, that is, its style. For that reason, understanding a work of art begins with a sensitive appreciation of its surface.

(In fact, art can be enjoyed for its purely visual appeal.) The word *style* is derived from stilus, the writing tool of the ancient Romans. Originally, it referred to distinctive ways of writing—the shape of the letters as well as the choice of words. Today it refers to the distinctive way in which a thing is done. In the visual arts, style means the specific way in which the forms that make up any given work of art are chosen and fitted together. To art historians the study of styles is of great importance. Not only does it enable them to find out, through careful analysis and comparison, when, where, and by whom something was produced, it also leads them to understand the artist's intention as expressed in the way it looks. This intention depends on both the artist's personality and the context of time and place. Thus art historians often speak of "period styles."

Art, like language, requires that we learn the style and outlook of a country, period, and artist if it is to be understood properly. Style need only be appropriate to the intent of the work. This idea is not always easy to accept. Westerners are used to a tradition of naturalism, in which art imitates nature as closely as possible. But accurate reproduction of visual phenomena, called illusionism, is just one means of expressing an artist's understanding of reality. Truth, it seems, is indeed relative. It is a matter not simply of what our eyes tell us but also of the concepts through which our perceptions are filtered. An image is a separate and self-contained reality that has its own ends and responds to its own rules as determined by the artist's creativity. Even the most convincing illusion is the product of the artist's imagination and understanding, so that we must always ask why this subject was chosen and expressed in this way rather than in some other way.

Self-Expression and Audience

The birth of a work of art is a very private experience, so much so that many artists can work only when they are alone and refuse to show their unfinished works to anyone. Yet for the birth to be successful, the work must be shared with the public. Artists do not create art just to satisfy themselves. They want their work validated by others. In fact, the creative process is not completed until the work has found an audience. In the end, works of art exist in order to be liked rather than to be debated. This paradox can be resolved once we understand what artists mean by "public." They are concerned not with the public at large but with their particular public, their audience. What matters to them is quality rather than wide approval. This audience is a limited and specialized one. Its members may be other artists as well as patrons, friends, critics, and interested viewers. What they all have in common is an informed love of works of art—an attitude that is at once discriminating and enthusiastic which lends particular weight to their judgments. They are, in a word, experts, people whose authority rests on experience and knowledge (see the cartoon on this page).

Tastes

The road to expertise in art is open to anyone who wants to take it. All that is required is an open mind and a capacity to absorb new experiences. The biggest roadblock is the old saying, "I don't know much about art, but I know what I like." When they say, "I know what I like," people really mean, "I like what I know [and I am uncomfortable with whatever is unfamiliar]." Such likes are not products of personal choice; they are imposed by habit and culture. Art is part of the fabric of our daily life; we see it all the time, even if only in the form of magazine covers, advertising posters, war memorials, television, and the buildings where we live, work, and worship. Much of this art, to be sure, is pretty shoddy, representing the common denominator of popular taste. Still, it is art of a sort, and since it is the only art most people experience, it molds their ideas about art in general. When faced with unfamiliar art, they often ask, "Why is that art?" when what they really mean is, "Why is that good art?" Deciding what is art and rating a work of art are two separate problems. Even if there were a tried-and-true way of distinguishing art from non-art, it would not necessarily help in measuring quality. Even so, people tend to combine these two problems into one.

But isn't the average person's opinion just as valid as an expert's? This notion has strong appeal in a democratic society. Let's see if it holds up to closer scrutiny. Take any subject in which you have some expertise. It might be sports, cars, carpentry, fashion, pop music. If I happen to be ignorant in the same area, is my judgment really as good as yours? Of course not! The expert always has the edge. As you also know from your own experience, having expertise in a subject greatly increases your enjoyment. The same is true of art. As their understanding grows, most people find themselves liking many more things than they had thought possible. They gradually acquire the courage of their own convictions, until they are able to say, with some justice, that they know what they like.

LOOKING AT ART

How we experience art has changed greatly over the course of history. To view art, most people go to museums. Museums, however, are a relatively recent invention. Although the Akropolis in Athens included a pinakotheke, or painting gallery, the idea of a museum ("home of the muses") where the public can go for inspiration arose only in the early nineteenth century. Before then, most people could see art only in churches. Except in seventeenth-century Holland, only wealthy collectors, most often members of the aristocracy, could afford to own art. Today museums have become temples where anyone can worship at the altar of art. Of course, most works of art were not created for such a setting. The art in museums is not the only kind worth looking at. On the contrary, it should provide the point of departure for exploring other forms of art.

Books like this one can serve as a guide to art, but no text or reproduction can substitute for viewing original works, even in an era when the written word has higher status than artists and their works. To those who love art, few pursuits are more pleasurable. A major benefit is being able to understand cartoons about art, since their humor is not obvious to everyone. Finding the cartoon on this page amusing requires knowing the painting entitled *The Scream* by Edvard Munch (see fig. 23-21). Learning to look at art is not an easy task, however, for art has become commonplace. We live in a sea of images that convey the culture and learning of modern civilization. Fueled by the mass media, this "visual background noise" has become so much a part of our daily lives that we take it for granted. In the process, we have become desensitized to art as well. Anyone can buy cheap paintings and reproductions to decorate a room, where they often hang unnoticed, perhaps deservedly so. It is small wonder that we look at the art in museums with equal casualness. We pass quickly from one object to another, sampling them like dishes in a cafeteria line. We may pause briefly before a famous masterpiece that we have been told we are supposed to admire.

But we are likely to ignore the equally beautiful and important works around it. We will have seen the art but not really looked at it.

Looking at great art is not an easy task, for art rarely reveals its secrets at first glance. While the experience of a work can be electrifying, we sometimes do not realize its impact until it has had time to filter through our imagination. It even happens that something which at first repelled or confused us emerges many years later as one of the most important artistic events of our lives. If we are going to get the most out of art, we will have to learn how to look and think for ourselves in an intelligent way, which is perhaps the hardest task of all. After all, we will not always have someone at our side to help us. In the end, the confrontation of viewer and art remains as solitary an act as making it.

Art represents the play between artists' imaginations and their surroundings. It also provides a personal record of life as it has been experienced by people at very different times and places. Because so much goes into art, it makes many of the same demands on us that it did on the person who created it. For that reason, we must be able to respond to a work on many levels. To understand it therefore requires a knowledge of both art history and life. The two go hand in hand. The more one knows about one, the more one can appreciate the other.

What people get out of art varies greatly from person to person. We each have different talents. Just as some people have a special ability in athletics or a knack for fixing things, others have a bent for spirituality or philosophy, or they may possess a historical imagination or a playful mind. Moreover, we each have different backgrounds and experiences. Thus we bring different skills to bear on looking at art, just as artists do in making it. Variety is indeed the spice of life. The world would be a dull place if everyone had the same views and backgrounds. Fortunately, there is room for almost limitless diversity. At the same time, there are broad common denominators, including culture and tradition, that bind us together just as much as human nature itself does.

APPROACHES TO ART HISTORY

The art historical approach of this book is often labeled *formalistic* insofar as it is concerned with the evolution of style. Thus it is akin to connoisseurship, although this should not be taken to mean the visual analysis of aesthetic qualities. It also draws on *iconography*, that is, the meaning of a work of art, and what art historian Erwin Panofsky called *iconology*, its cultural context. This book takes a classical approach to art history as defined by three generations of mainly German-born scholars—including H. W. Janson, a student of Panofsky. It is well suited to introducing beginners to art history by providing the framework for how to look at and respond to art in museums and galleries—something both authors have greatly enjoyed throughout their lives. In nearly every case, the works illustrated here (or very similar ones) have been seen by one or both authors to be certain that they are indeed worthy of inclusion. In some cases we have changed our minds, especially when it comes to recent art that has not had the benefit of time to gain the historical perspective needed for a full appraisal.

Readers should be aware that there are other approaches. The oldest is Marxism, which views art in terms of the social and political conditions determined by the prevailing economic system. Marxist analysis has been especially useful in treating art since the Industrial Revolution, which created the conditions that were analyzed by Karl Marx in the mid-nineteenth century. It remains to be seen what will become of Marxist art history in the wake of the collapse of Communism in Russia and Eastern Europe.

Psychology, too, has added many insights into the meaning works of art have for their creators, particularly when that meaning is hidden even from the artists themselves. The more extreme attempts to psychoanalyze Leonardo and Michelangelo, for instance, have caused some scholars to distrust this method. But some works, such as Fuseli's *The Nightmare* (whose meaning was analyzed by H. W. Janson in a pioneering article), cannot be understood without it.

Three newer approaches—feminism, multiculturalism, and deconstruction—are perhaps the most radical of all. Feminism reexamines art history from the point of view of gender. Because this approach is embedded in current gender politics, there is a risk that a major shift in social outlook might call some of feminism's conclusions into question. In principle, however, feminist theory can be applied to all of art history. It certainly forces us to reconsider what is "good" art. After all, when this book first appeared, not a single woman artist was included—nor was one to be found in any other art history survey. Today such omissions seem nothing short of unthinkable.

Feminism is related to the larger shift toward multiculturalism, which addresses the gap in our understanding of the art of nontraditional and non-Western cultures. Why should we not include artists who express very different sensibilities from that of the European and American mainstream? Indeed, there is no reason whatsoever not to. However; this book is limited to Western art for both practical and philosophical reasons. I have chosen instead to focus on the contribution of African-American art. In the process, however, I have taken a stand about what art is most important that not all readers will agree with, since it favors universalism over ethnocentrism. In part, this reflects my own views on the stereotyping ethnocentrism fosters on both sides of the racial fence. In my opinion, such an approach is doomed as a cultural dead end, although I cannot deny that art with a racial "edge" has a legitimate place. Feminism and multiculturalism have both attacked the "canon" of masterpieces in this and similar books as embodying male chauvinism and colonialist attitudes. Readers should judge the issue for themselves. I would only point out that one must walk before one can run.

Because they are so central to postmodern thought, semiotics and deconstruction are briefly summarized toward the end of the book. I am sympathetic to semiotics, which I first became interested in more than 20 years ago, although I find Noam Chomsky's theory of linguistics more satisfying. Deconstruction has likewise made art historians consider meaning in new ways that have breathed fresh life into the field. Nevertheless, I know from classroom experience that it is nearly impossible for beginning art history students to understand semiotics. Deconstruction is even more taxing. What began as a feud between two schools of French semiologists has spread to art history, where it pits older, mostly German-trained scholars against a younger generation. And perhaps that is the point. People are constantly reinventing art history in their image. But if art history reflects our times, the reader may wonder how it can have any claim to objectivity and, hence, validity. In fact, people's understanding of history has always changed with the times. How could it be otherwise? It seems almost necessary for each generation to reinvent history so that we may understand both the past and the present. Yet the danger is that ideology, regardless of its noble intent, will undermine the search for truth, no matter how relative truth may be. Such a thing happened during the 1930s, when scholarship was made to serve the political ends of dictatorships—which led Panofsky and Janson to leave Germany.

Neither author of *History of Art* is an ideologue. Both are (in the case of my father, were) humanists who believe that the study of humane letters is enjoyable and enriching. Such a view requires that scholarly discourse be temperate, although it is rarely dispassionate. I would encourage the reader to examine all forms of art history with an open mind. One cannot view something as rich and complex as art from a single perspective any more than it is possible to see a diamond from a single vantage point. Each approach can add to our understanding. To be sure, a plea for tolerance may seem outdated at a time when art history, like all fields, has become so contentious. In this regard, scholarship reflects the rapid political change, social unrest, ideological dogmatism, and religious fanaticism that characterize postindustrial society and the new world order that is emerging in its wake. Let all ideas meet the test of the marketplace of ideas, where they can be discussed openly and fairly. Let us also allow everyone to tend his own intellectual garden in peace. Some may have a larger plot than others, but even the biggest of them is rather small in the scheme of things, as H. W. Janson, among the most famous art historians of his time, came to understand.

Both authors have given a great deal of thought to this book, which is written in the authoritative tones that intellectuals habitually adopt as their public voice. It is difficult, of course, to resist the temptation to pontificate—to hand down the "canon" as if it were immutable. Yet, if the truth be told, the experience of surveying such a broad field as art history provides a lesson in humility. One becomes only too aware of the painful omissions and how little one knows about any given subject in this age of increasing specialization. If it requires the egotism of the gods to undertake such a project in the first place, in the end one sees it clearly for what it is: an act of hubris. It also requires a faith in the power of reason to produce such a synthesis, something that is in short supply these days.

History of Art: Primer of Art History

The Introduction to this book, which begins on page 39, has been written by H. W. Janson and Anthony F. Janson over a period of more than 40 years. Although presented as a deceptively simple narrative, the Introduction is actually a gathering of eloquent linked essays, some of which explore questions that are among the most meaningful we could be asked: What is art? What is essential to the creation of art? What makes a visual artist different from other people? Why does an artist make art? Does it matter whether anyone besides the artist sees and experiences the things an artist creates? Is your opinion as good as the next person's?

These questions have many possible responses and, wisely, the Jansons ask us to try to answer them for ourselves, with as much authenticity as we can summon.

This brief Primer of Art History, by contrast, does not ask profound questions. Its two purposes are quite plain. One is to introduce you to the field of art history as a humanistic discipline. The other is to provide you with a set of basic tools to take with you on your journey with art from prehistory to the present.

The oldest surviving expressions of human culture are prehistoric. Almost 90,000 years ago, human beings began fashioning and decorating beads—evidence of symbolic thinking—and they had been shaping specialized tools far longer. Recent genetic studies suggest that spoken languages probably developed more than 50,000 years ago. Then, about 30,000 years ago, our ancestors began painting subtly expressive images of animals on the walls of caves in southern Europe. Thus the tangible evidence we have of our distant ancestors' lives and values is their handiwork and their art. When you study art history, from the very beginning you are engaging with real objects of human experience. As the Jansons' Introduction says so eloquently, however, art objects are not ordinary, forced-by-necessity creations, but are things made to satisfy uniquely human aspirations and longings.

The Field

Art history is a relatively new field of study compared, for example, to literature and philosophy. In the United States, art history began to flourish as a scholarly discipline and a college and university curriculum only in the twentieth century, and mostly after World War II. (Technology affected art history's late start, because until the advent of photography and of printing technologies that could reproduce images cheaply enough to circulate widely, it was rare for one person to see, remember, and compare a great number of physical objects—to say nothing of publishing illustrated books and articles about art.) Art appreciation, which is taught at colleges and universities and is an important component of museum education programs, invariably includes some art history in the process of exposing and sensitizing us to visual culture. Likewise, art history's more rigorous and systematic study of art across time inevitably ignites a lifelong appreciation of the objects of study.

ART HISTORIANS. Men and women who 'devote their lives to the study of art are called art historians. Most art historians have advanced degrees, and most are passionate and articulate about art and ideas. This edition of *History of Art* draws attention to these qualities in 24 extended captions that capture the rigor, passion, and curiosity of some of this century's most distinguished art historians.

What, besides teaching, do art historians do? Some research and write, thus contributing to art history's body of knowledge or disseminating what is known to a wider audience. Others are museum professionals: curators, administrators, archivists, and conservators. Fewer independent experts advise museums and collectors about acquisitions. Some gallery owners and staff are art historians, and so are a number of publishing professionals, especially editors. What they all share is a pervading sense of excitement about the object of their attention, art.

APPROACHES. Like all fields of inquiry, art history has undergone some fundamental changes. For a long time, art history was confined to the so-called fine arts of painting, sculpture, and architecture. Drawing and the graphic arts—works printed on paper—were also included. Stained glass and decorated (illuminated) manuscripts were regarded as painting, and so qualified as fine art. Photography was admitted to the field of study a few decades ago. More recently, art historians have expanded the definition of art to include works in many mediums (*mediums*, not *media*, is the art historian's preferred plural; medium is the material the artist uses to make the artwork). Today textiles and other fiber arts, metalworking and silver-and goldsmithery, ceramics, glass, beadwork, and mixed mediums are in art history's realm. Modern and contemporary art, especially, has forced open the borders by constantly questioning and expanding the range. Happenings (one-time performed creations staged by artists in the 1950s), earth art, video art, performance art, installations, computer art, and almost anything selected by an artist and declared to be art are now generally acknowledged to be forms of art-making.

Not all art historians approach the subject the same way. Some concentrate on *connoisseurship*: the way art looks. They note and savor visual elements—such as line, color, shape, mass—and the materials and techniques the artist used to create a work of art, then analyze how these were brought together to achieve a certain appearance and have a certain effect. The visual elements are referred to as *formal elements*, and the term *formalism* denotes art history that emphasizes the art object per se, comparatively independent of historical and other non-artistic influences. A formalist looks first and foremost to other artworks to find the answers to why something looks the way it does and what the artist meant by it.

Clearly allied to formalism is *iconography*, the description of images and the study of their meanings, which includes decoding visual symbols (see below, "Symbols"). *Iconology*, which is related to iconography, is the science of images' meanings synthesized with insights from many other fields, such as psychology, sociology, and economics; this process greatly expands the context of any work's creation—and thus possibility for larger interpretation of its meaning. Iconography and iconology were for many years a mainstream tradition of art history. Only recently have they shared the stage with newer schools that view art history from the vantage points of gender, nationality, politics, social criticism, and the humanistic disciples. The most important of these are discussed at the end of the Introduction.

Art historians who take into consideration what was happening at the time and place of an artwork's creation to explain why a work looks the way it does are practicing *contextualism* and are known as *contextualist* art historians. They explore questions such as: What do we know about the artist? Who had political and economic power at the time? Who paid for artworks, and what were the motives of these people, called patrons? What ideas were circulating in educated circles at the time? Today, most art history, including Janson's *History of Art*, is a fusion of formalism and contextualism.

Where Will You Find Art?

The answer is, "Almost everywhere." We can experience it first-hand or secondhand. Museums are obvious places for face-to-face encounters with the real thing. However, art sheltered in museums is separated from the original context of its creation, whether dug from the site of a long-buried civilization, taken from a church or palace, or even removed from the living room wall of a wealthy collector One of the pleasures of studying art history is that it equips us to re-create the contexts, which we bring to bear on art wherever we find art: painted on the inside walls of caves, built as architectural sites all over the world, carved into rock, laid into floors, woven into special garments, erected in parks and malls, installed in corporate offices and private dwellings, and now, winking at us from computer screens.

When we look at reproductions of art, as we do in illustrated books, journals, magazines, posters, and notecards, in the darkened classroom, and on CDs, dedicated websites, and the Internet, we trade quantity for quality. Only real objects can tell us size and scale, true color and texture, and can reveal aesthetic attributes too subtle to capture except by direct experience. Still, most of us begin our relationship with art through the medium of reproductions, invariably accompanied by words.

The Specialized Vocabulary of Art

The fundamental quality of art is visual and/or spatial. We need to "read" art and architecture in their terms. To do so, however, it is almost essential to master and use the vocabulary and grammar that have been devised to help convert the visual experience into the common currency of language. We need to accept the premise that words are symbolic translations of the visual experience, which is a powerful and direct transaction between eye and mind. Much of the great power of images lies in that fact.

The better we understand the specialized vocabulary, grammar, and syntax of art history, the more we benefit from the work of people who spend their lives looking at and making sense of art. Art historians and critics are, after all, attempting to bring order and meaning to this vast—and specialized—form of human expression.

BASIC TERMINOLOGY. Both two-dimensional art (paintings and works of graphic art, for example) and three-dimensional sculpture rely on descriptors such as *representational, realistic, abstract,* and *nonobjective* to broadly categorize an artist's visual approach to a subject. **Representational art** has subject matter that is recognizable from the natural world. **Realistic art** shows a high degree of imitation, or verisimilitude, of the actual objects or subject. **Abstract art** simplifies and alters the appearance of actual forms (they can still be recognizable) for various purposes, often to suggest an essence or universality. **Nonobjective art** deals with

forms that lack any reference to the natural world. Also referred to as **nonrepresentational** or **nonfigurative**, it relies solely on the interplay of formal visual elements. Much modern art is nonobjective.

FORMAL ELEMENTS. What are the formal elements? They include *line, shape, mass,* and *color,* as well as texture and composition. **Line** can be drawn to define outlines, edges, and contours of forms and delineating shapes. Line imparts direction and movement, even when it is not a continuous mark. Implied lines, which our eyes seek out and our brains mentally connect, can be pictorially as effective as an actual, continuous line.

Shape is a two-dimensional form, an area on a flat plane. **Form** is three-dimensional, occupying a volume of space. Sculpture that is freestanding is **mass**. So is architecture. But you experience architecture by moving around, into, and through it, not merely around it, as you have to do with sculpture.

Texture and color, which are activated by light, are the two other most important formal elements. Texture can refer to the actual surface quality of a work of art or architecture or to the surface that the artist has imitated.

Full understanding of color lies in the realm of physics. **Color** is the effect on our brains of light of differing wavelengths reflected off objects. The source light is usually white light, which is a combination of all colors. Objects absorb particular parts of white light, while reflecting others, so that they give the optical impression of having a particular color. It is helpful to understand the meaning of three color-related terms when you are reading about art. They are *hue, value,* and *intensity.* **Hue** refers to the essential color. The visible colors of a rainbow are the so-called spectral hues of red, orange, yellow, green, blue-violet and violet. In the case of a rainbow, when the white light of the sun passes through drops of water in the air, the raindrops become like crystal prisms that separate wavelengths of light into the spectral hues.

Value refers to the degree of lightness or darkness of a color. Two additional terms are sometimes used when describing value. One is **tint**, a color lighter than the hue's normal value, and the other is **shade**, a color darker than normal. Thus, apple green is a tint of pure green, and forest green in a shade. Finally, there is the term **intensity** (also called *saturation* or *chroma*). Intensity is the degree of a hue's purity. The closer a color is to the original rainbow-spectrum hue, the higher its intensity and the brighter its appearance.

THE ILLUSION OF SPACE. Artists working in two-dimensional arts are challenged with representing the real world of three-dimensionality on a flat plane. The flat surface, termed the **picture plane**, is the field on which the artist builds the illusion of space and three-dimensionality. **Picture space** is a term for what is created in that illusion. Artists have devised many pictorial strategies for suggesting space and objects in space, among them: **vertical** stacking of forms, the **overlapping** of forms, and the illusion of distance by gradation of color from intense to pale, often bluish hues (**atmospheric** or **aerial perspective**).

Since the Italian Renaissance in the fifteenth century, the Western tradition has settled on **scientific**, or **linear, perspective** as the most satisfactory method. It is based on two observations. One is that forms look smaller the farther away they are, and the other is that parallel lines (such as railroad tracks) appear to converge and vanish at the point in the distance where sky meets earth. Scientific perspective assumes the artist's (and viewer's) fixed position and one or more **vanishing points** on a **horizon line**.

Another way artists suggest three-dimensionality is with the depiction of **light**. It is, after all, light that allows us to perceive forms. In the dark, form is invisible. By manipulating the range from light to dark, called the *value scale*, artists can define forms by suggesting shadow, and they tell us where the light source is.

COMPOSITION. The way an artist puts the formal elements together is called **composition**. Whether it be a painting, a sculpture, or even a work of architecture, composition is distinctive from artists to artist and from culture to culture. Composition is one of the most closely studied attributes of an artwork, especially in formalist art history, because composition is one of the most revealing dimensions of style in a work of art.

STYLE. The word *style* used in art history is different from other, more general uses for the word. With art, it describes the combination of distinguishing characteristics that imprint a work of art as the creation of a certain artist, or time, or place. As the Jansons say so eloquently in their Introduction, "To art historians the study of styles is of central importance. It not only enables them to find out, by means of careful analysis and comparison, when, where, and often by whom a given work was produced, but it also leads them to understand the artist's intention as expressed through the style of the work."

SUBJECT MATTER. What else reveals the artist's intention? **Subject matter**—so to speak, the topic of an artwork—is an obvious clue to intention. Although the choice is always significant in itself, subject matter is neutral. But the way the artist handles the subject is infinitely variable and is not neutral. Subject matter does not need to be pictorially recognizable. An artist intending to create an expression of grief, for example, has many choices, from making a realistic portrayal of a person grieving the death of a loved one, to a totally nonobjective,. subjective evocation of the emotional state of grief. The subject matter will be the same. The appearance, or form, will be utterly different.

SYMBOLS. For as long as people have been making images, they have been devising and using pictorial **symbols** to represent abstract ideas or abstract dimensions of real objects. The earliest written languages employ pictographic symbols to stand for objects and ideas; Egyptian hieroglyphics are examples of this. The evangelists of New Testament theology are often represented by symbols: an angel or human being for Matthew, a lion for Mark, a steer for Luke, and an eagle for John. At this level, these images can be either symbols for the individual evangelists or, when shown in connection with a picture of an evangelist, an **attribute**, or visual identifier of the figure in the picture. Symbols constitute a language of their own, and iconography, one of art history's most fascinating sub-disciplines, is devoted to exploring their meaning.

The centaur—the part human/part horse creature of ancient Greek mythology—is symbolic in a different way. One of its references is to the dual nature of man: the wild and irrational alongside the rationally self-controlled. Another is to the body/mind duality and conflict so prevalent in Western thinking.

FORM AND CONTENT. Symbols are form. Their meaning is an aspect of content. **Form** is what we see in a work of art, what is visible. It is indisputable. What we interpret from the form is called **content**—the message or meaning of the work. The content of the realistic and the nonrepresentational images of grief mentioned above will vary for every single viewer, not just because the forms are different but because every person brings a different set of experiences, emotional makeup, cultural conditioning, and kinds of knowledge to his or her experience.

Content is nourished by whatever knowledge we can bring to our encounters with works of art, including knowing the times and places of their creation, having an understanding of style, and possessing an informed notion of what the artist intended to say. But it is also fed by life itself. It is safe to say that the more you know about life, the more you know about art, because you bring broader and richer experience to your encounters.

Museum Labels and Illustration Captions

Museums as places where the general public can go to see and learn more about art are a relatively recent invention. As permanent as they seem today, museums as we know them did not exist before the eighteenth century. The same is true of privately owned galleries, which sell works of art. Art museums are as large as The Metropolitan Museum of Art in New York City or Musée du Louvre (the Louvre) in Paris and as small as a one-or two-room exhibition space associated with a college or university to house a small or specialized collection.

What almost all museums have in common is a strong educational component, including a lot of explanatory written material: illustrated catalogues and labels and informative interpretations (wall texts) that appear in proximity to artworks. In addition, most museum have websites.

Museum labels and **illustration captions** in a book such as this one use specialized conventions:

1 Name of artist. Usually given first name first, the artist's name is followed by nationality and life dates. From the information in this label, we learn that although Duchamp was born in France, the Philadelphia Museum of Art refers to him as American. (In fact, he did spend many decades of his long life in the U.S.)

2 Name of work. The Philadelphia Museum of Art is among a slowly growing number of institutions to place the title of the work before the name of the artist.

The title a museum gives to a work in its possession is considered authoritative and should be used. When titles are changed, it is usually because research has revealed important reasons to rename a work.

3 Date of work. The date of creation usually follows the name of the work.

4 Material. The medium is oil paint on canvas. Technique will be given when it is relevant. An example would be "cast bronze."

5 Dimensions. Size is sometimes given and sometimes omitted in museum labels. Dimensions in a caption are given height before width before depth, often in both imperial (inches/feet) and metric (centimeters/meters) measure. Size is deceiving in reproductions. Measurements are less critical to have when one is standing in front of the original.

6 Donor or collection information. While not essential information to identifying the work of art, the names of the donors who gave the work to the institution—or donated funds used to purchase it—are part of the work's history. Museums want to credit the generosity of donors, who are vital to the health of the institution.

7 Accession number. Invariably the last item of information on a museum label, the accession number is a unique identifying code. Usually, it includes the year the work came into the collection, in this case, 1950.

8 Copyright information. More and more, as copyright of artworks is claimed by institutions, heirs of artists, and image providers, copyright information appears in illustration captions. This copyright line indicates that Succession Marcel Duchamp holds copyright of this image and is represented by Artist Rights Society, New York (ARS, NY).

Some museums provide additional information and interpretation in the form of **wall text**. When an installation has a lot of written information on the walls, it almost begins to replicate the experience of reading an art book. In that case, the challenge to us is how to balance our attention between the artwork and the information about it.

JULIA MOORE
January 2003

# 4 Architecture

Writing About Art and Architecture: Architecture

Like paintings, sculptures, and works of literature, works of architecture can be viewed in relation to their time and place of construction. In fact, works of architecture, because they are made for a practical purpose, must be considered in relation to the societies reponsible for producing them. The question is less academic than practical.

A work of architecture, such as a church or a public building, can be considered from the standpoint of its purpose or function—why it was made; its structural soundness—how well it is made; and its design—how beautifully it has been made. We take up these three essential architectural aspects briefly, one at a time.

First, purpose. Was the work constructed for a single specific purpose, as for example a Buddhist temple or a Gothic cathedral for worship? Has the original purpose of the building been supplanted by another at a later period, as for example converting a ruler's palace into a legislative assembly hall or a museum? Has the building been expanded, contracted, remodeled, renovated, restored, or in any way altered? If so, with what results?

How does the building fit into its surrounding context—its neighborhood, its building site? Is it integrated into its surroundings, or does it stand out from them? Was this the original intention of the architect? To what extent have its surroundings changed? How well is it related to other buildings and structures that have been erected since it was constructed?

Second, structure. How solidly is it built? Has it held up over time? Is it structurally sound? To what extent do its interior spaces fit the purposes for which they were originally designed? That is, to what extent does form follow function? To what extent might the form be symbolic—representing tranquillity or energy, for example?

Of what materials is it made? What associations do its materials have—marble and granite suggest power and prestige, durability and dignity. Wood is humbler but can suggest simplicity and rusticity if left "natural," and if smoothly sanded and painted, something more communal, perhaps more "finished."

Third, design. It perhaps seems strange to ask what a building suggests or expresses in the way we might consider a sculpture or a painting expressive. Nonetheless, a building's size and scale, its shape and form, color and texture, speak to the same kinds of aesthetic issues and responses that works of art do. What does a structure's design contribute to its "meaning"?

And, more specifically, you can ask other kinds of questions about architectural structures:

Guidelines for Analyzing Architecture

- Is it ornamented or decorated in any way, and if so, how, and to what effect? How are its interior spaces arranged, divided, allocated?
- What are its walls and floors made of—brick? wood? marble? To what effect?
- What colors are its walls and floors and ceilings?
- Does the building seem warm and inviting? Or does it seem cold and forbidding? Why?
- How is it lighted? What place does natural daylight have in its design? What aesthetic effect does light—both natural and artificial—have on the overall feeling the building creates?
- To what extent does the building represent either a particular individual's architectural philosophy or a sociocultural architectural style or perspective?
- To what extent does the building reflect the architectural style from an earlier era? To what purpose, and with what effect?

An Architectural Proposal

The following essay—an op ed piece published in the *Wall Street Journal*—argues for the inclusion of a large open-air theater as part of the architectural concept for the site of the former World Trade Center. The writer, Joan Breton Connelly, a professor of art history, does not put forth a complete architectural proposal for the site. Rather, she explains why a particular kind of open-air theater should be included as part of the plan.

Let's Look to Ancient Forms for a Memorial

Joan Breton Connelly

Beginning in the sixth century B.C., Athenians gathered on the south slope of the Acropolis to watch the great dramatic works that have survived to this day. In time, the Athenians' Theater of Dionysos grew to seat some 15,000 viewers who regularly came to participate in dramatic festivals that gave emotional catharsis to their lives.

So central was theater to the ancient Greek experience that it became a required component of every Greek city plan. When Alexander the Great marched eastward, founding over 70 cities, each aspired to boast a council house, a temple, a stadium and, importantly, a theater. Even at Kandahar and Bagram in distant Afghanistan, Greek theaters rose to embrace and enthrall scores of viewers, binding them together in a meaningful communal experience.

Among the very highest honors awarded to an Athenian citizen was the right to have his or her name inscribed upon a seat in the city's theater. Politicians, generals, and others of distinction were granted the privilege by which generations that followed could read and remember the names of those who had contributed so mightily to their community.

To this day we can see the names of those who died over 2,000 years ago. We know nothing of the life of a priestess named Athenion who served in A.D. 134. But when we run our fingers across her name, engraved on a seat that still stands in 21st-century Athens, she is present to us across the ages.

Today, as we follow the important and necessary debate over what should be built at Ground Zero, we participate in a discussion that is as old as humankind itself. At the very core of the debate are some strikingly profound tensions: those between creativity and memory, freedom and discipline, imagination, and will.

We should consider, as at least one component of the rebuilding, the possibility of a World Trade Center Memorial Theater. Imagine an open-air theater, with a sweeping semicircular grandstand of at least 3000 seats, one inscribed for each life lost on Sept. 11. The viewer would look down from the great expanse of benches into the orchestra, a circular stage area below and its backdrop: that great stretch of exterior wall salvaged from the ruins of the Trade Towers just weeks after the attack.

A theater is defined by the experience of its viewers. It shifts and changes with the events that occur within its embrace. A

Memorial Theater could be a place of quiet contemplation, where loved ones would visit the inscribed names of the lost, sit and remember and look down upon the surviving bit of superstructure that bears witness to their suffering. It could also be a place of public oratory for the countless memorials that will consecrate that day and site for generations to come. All the while, it could be a place for workers to bring their brown bag lunches and rest as they once did at the World Trade Center Plaza.

By night, the theater would come alive with the sounds of symphonies and well-loved arias, with age-old tragedies and heart-lifting comedies, with rock bands and film festivals, and circus flyers and displays of the imagination, creativity and energy that make this city so vibrant. Flooded in wintertime, the orchestra space would metamorphose into a skating rink, a source of endless smiles for those watching from the bleachers.

Our Memorial Theater would provide a final destination for that most quintessential of New York institutions: the ticker tape parade. Here, the great processions through Wall Street would culminate in ceremonies celebrating our most esteemed sports stars, astronauts, and future heroes against the backdrop of the very last surviving piece of the Trade Towers ruin. And in thus transforming the World Trade Center site into the centerpiece of the recreational and commemorative life of the city, we would be declaring: The terrorists did not win.

The finest memorial for the dead is life itself. Let those who perished communally, a throng of some 3,000 taken from us in a single day, be honored through a never-ending chorus of the living. A theater filled with exhilarated and inspired, entertained and contemplative Americans encircled in one of the oldest architectural forms given to us by those who invented democracy itself.

A Memorial Theater could accommodate the thousands of world visitors who most certainly will make pilgrimages to the site. On its very uppermost level, along the broad arc that encircles the sweeping seating space below, let us fly high the flags of every nation that lost a citizen in the Sept. 11 attack. When the world visits our most devastating national shrine let them know that we have remembered their children, too. And let them know that we have responded to this unspeakable destruction with the most powerful answer of all, life.

Reprinted by permission from the *Wall Street Journal*, October 17, 2002.

Joan Breton Connelly is an associate professor of fine arts at New York University.

EXERCISE

Analyze the argument made by Professor Connelly for an open-air theater as part of the rebuilding scheme for the World Trade Center. Then write two paragraphs, first summarizing her views, and then responding to them. You can agree, disagree, or qualify her argument in your response to her.

Student Essay on Architecture

In the following paper, Emily Sheeler, a student, compares the influence of the Egyptian temples at Luxor and Karnak with that of the Greek Parthenon.

Influence through Architecture

For centuries temples and statues have been constructed to pay homage to gods of many cultures. Although they vary in size, construction, and technique, they serve as an intertwining thread that links seemingly disconnected time periods and cultures. Through art it is possible to see influence and commingling from other cultures; art proves to be one of the most influential aspects of history that sews together communities that may otherwise have never been connected. The one binding factor that helps lead to a connection through art is that of faith. Gods have always been a prevalent aspect in most, if not all, cultures and have even caused wars, destruction, and untimely downfalls. The influence of the gods can be seen in historical texts but through art in all its forms as well—in Homer's *The Odyssey*, Virgil's *The Aeneid,* and certainly through architecture. Some of the most well known art pieces and structures were created to praise some god or gods. Not only were these pieces painstakingly constructed over many years to please the gods but also, although unknowingly, to influence the cultures and techniques that came after them. The building of the Temples at Luxor and Karnak by the Egyptians are not only to be marveled at but also to be examined and thought of as a piece of history that influenced the construction of other even more well known structures, such as the Parthenon.

The building of the massive structures at Luxor and Karnak are proof themselves of the influence of previous art on culture and new art. These temples replaced smaller ones that were begun during

the Middle Kingdom. The innate urge to display power and triumph
can find no better medium than art. The rather thinly veiled idea
that these structures were created to praise a god (Amun), although
this does hold some truth, is largely outweighed by the fact that
their creation was a show of power. "As an expression of pharaonic
power, the temples at Luxor and Karnak are without equal" (Janson
47). However, it was not only power over the current civilization
that prompted these pharaohs to build such a massive and imposing
structure, but the influence that they would have over future cultures. Power is intoxicating and one of the few things that can
transcend time; this is an idea that the Egyptians were very well
aware of in building these temples. The temples themselves were
built on "a principle of exclusion" (Janson 46), which shows that
they were meant to stand apart and be noticed as structures to be
reckoned with just as was the government.

The temples were made so as to be shown in the best light not
from an outside perspective but rather from one who is inside the
temple. This speaks highly of the Egyptians' need to control and
conquer. The worshippers were almost confined in this temple,
afraid even that the weighty structure would cause their death.
Fear was a primary motivator in this architectural feat; in fact
the architect purposely made the weight of the columns in the
structure heavier than needed. This overwhelming sense of power and
fear casts the praising of the gods in a shadowed light; portraying
power as the most important aspect of culture, rather than worship.

This unbridled urge for power and influence was not lost on the
Greeks. In achieving their greatest architectural feat, and possibly the best known historical structure the world, the Parthenon,
power played a great role. Much like the Egyptians' temples, the
Parthenon was set high on a hill and away from the ordinary. It was
constructed for the goddess Athena, ironically the Greek goddess of
war and wisdom. The looming structure looks down on those in the
city from the Acropolis, almost spiting those below as underlings.
However, the structure is far less impending than others and offers
a sense of support rather than fear (as the Egyptian structure).
The time surely influenced the architects (Iktinos, Kallikrates,
and Kaprion) when creating the structure. The money raised to construct the site was taken from funds that had been received in

order to ward off the Persian enemy. This brazen move of taking funds out of money for defense only shows how far rulers will go to glorify not only themselves but their city.

Although the Parthenon is and will always be known as one of the greatest architectural feats in history, it ultimately was a helping factor in the downfall of Athens. It begs the question which is greater: longevity of a city or longevity of influence and power? Cleary, Perikles chose influence. There are few structures that come close to the fame of the Parthenon and this is ultimately what Perikles sacrificed his defense against the Persians for, endless fame and influence. At the time the Parthenon was constructed it was highly debated as whether or not it was worth what it cost them, as if the inhabitants of the city were aware of their untimely doom. Yet the Parthenon was something not suggesting an end, but was rather lively and intimate. Although the Egyptian influence can be seen in some aspects of the Parthenon, it varies in its overall sense.

The Parthenon was far more welcoming and open than the temples at Luxor and Karnak but this merely shows the progression of time. It was as if the rulers of these civilizations found a better way to exude power over their people and prolong their influence. The Egyptians thought it best to strike fear into the people's hearts, thus causing them to remain respectful not only of the current government but of the gods the temples were constructed for as well. This is a much different perspective than what the Greeks did with their Parthenon. The Parthenon was much more inviting and sought to rule through rank, being built on the highest point of the city, and friendship. The Greeks are often seen as a much livelier group of people, who celebrate food and wine when reveling in worship of their gods. The structure proves as a backdrop for the Grecian lifestyle. Regardless of how both civilizations sought to ooze power and influence, their goal was much the same: to be remembered through history as nations that were able to create menacing works of art.

The question of whether or not the two civilizations succeeded in their goal is debatable. If the Egyptians had not created such works of art like these temples, would they have been as well remembered? It is unlikely. Although history may be seen as the past, this cannot hold true in the world of architecture and art. The Egyptians created something that can never be forgotten. There is a sense of immortality in these temples that will surely never die as the Kingdoms did. The Greeks are the same way, known not only for their glorious history and very well known defeat, but also for the Parthenon.

There are few places in the world that this structure is not echoed in some sense through art. Influence is a tremendous idea, and both civilizations achieved greatly at this. The Egyptians surely influenced the building of the Parthenon and thus must always be remembered. Art, although it is beautiful and holds meanings that may never be fully discovered, is used as a medium for eternal influence. In the structure of the Parthenon can be seen traces of Egyptian influence: dominating the city as did the temples of Luxor and Karnak, showcasing power no matter what the cost, and having the same goal of ascendancy.

Power may be corrupting, but it can also be used for good. Looking at the art from a standpoint of beauty there is nothing lacking in these magnificent structures; they are strong and demanding while still aesthetically pleasing. It is the beauty of these structures that cause their timelessness, which is why their construction cost so much. It cost the Athenians their city, while the Egyptian temple only highlighted their unholy drive for power. It is ironic that the course of history would have the Greeks conquering the Egyptians. The Egyptian temples of Luxor and Karnak surely influenced the Athenian Parthenon, which was a factor in their downfall. The ties of influence never end, and both the Egyptian temples as well as the Parthenon only serve to further enforce this idea.

CRITICAL THINKING: *Monuments*

A perennially debated question for countries during and after wars is how to memorialize their dead. Following the Vietnam War, a debate ensued about how to best remember the Americans who died in Vietnam. A contest was held with over a thousand entries submitted, resulting in the selection of a design by Maya Lin, which has since become the Vietnam Veterans War Memorial, better known as "The Wall."

Lin's design for a monument was unconventional, departing radically from traditional realistic representations of soldiers in combat gear. Instead of depicting soldiers realistically in action, Lin opted for a more symbolic design, with a long, black, shiny granite wall incised with the names of all soldiers who died in the war. Why do you think some people opposed Lin's design for the monument, and preferred something more traditional? Why, after more than twenty years that the Vietnam Memorial has stood, do you think it has retained its popularity, having become the most visited of all memorials?

Perceiving the Arts: Architecture

Every street in our towns represents a museum of ideas and engineering. The houses, churches, and commercial buildings we pass every day reflect appearances and techniques that may be as old as the human race itself. We go in and out of these buildings, often without notice, and yet they engage us and frequently dictate actions we can or cannot take.

In approaching architecture as an art, we cannot separate aesthetic properties from practical or functional properties. In other words, architects first have a practical function to achieve in their buildings, which forms their principal concern. The aesthetics of the building remain important, but they must be tailored to overall practical considerations. For example, when architects set about to design a 110-story skyscraper, they are locked into a vertical rather than horizontal aesthetic form. They may attempt to counter verticality with strong horizontal elements, but the physical fact that the building will be taller than wide creates the basis from which the architects must work. Their structural design must take into account all the practical needs implicit in the building's use. Nonetheless, considerable room for aesthetics remains. Treatment of space, texture, line, and proportion can give us buildings of unique style and character or buildings of unimaginative sameness.

Architecture often is described as the art of sheltering. To consider it as such, we must use the term *sheltering* very broadly. Obviously, types of architecture exist within which people do not dwell and under which they cannot escape the rain. Architecture encompasses more than buildings. So, we can consider architecture as the art of sheltering people both physically and spiritually from the raw elements of the unaltered world.

WHAT IS IT?

As we noted, architecture can be considered the art of sheltering. In another large sense, it comprises the design of three-dimensional space to create practical enclosure. Its basic forms include residences, churches, and commercial buildings. Each of these forms can take innumerable shapes, from single-family residences to the ornate palaces of kings to high-rise condominiums and apartments. We also could expand our categorization of architectural forms to include bridges, walls, monuments, and so forth.

HOW IS IT PUT TOGETHER?

In examining how a work of architecture is put together, we limit ourselves to ten fundamental elements: structure, materials, line, repetition, balance, scale, proportion, context, space, and climate.

STRUCTURE

Many systems of construction or systems of structural support exist. We deal with only a few of the more prominent. *Post-and-lintel,*

arch, and *cantilever* systems can be viewed, essentially, as historical systems. Contemporary architecture, however, can better be described by two additional terms, which to some extent overlap the others. These contemporary systems are *bearing-wall* and *skeleton frame.*

Post-and-Lintel

Post-and-lintel structure (see Figs. 9.1 and 9.2) consists of horizontal beams (lintels) laid across the open spaces between vertical supports (posts). In this architectural system, the traditional material is stone. Post-and-lintel structure is similar to *post-and-beam* structure, in which series of vertical posts join horizontal members, traditionally of wood. The wooden members of post-and-beam structure are held together by nails, pegs, or lap joints.

Lack of tensile strength in its fundamental material, stone, limits post-and-lintel structure in its ability to define space. *Tensile strength* is the ability of a material to withstand bending. If we lay a slab of stone across an open space and support it only at each end, we can span only a narrow space before it cracks in the middle and falls to the ground. However, stone has great *compressive strength*—the ability to withstand compression or crushing.

A primitive example of post-and-lintel structure is Stonehenge, that ancient and mysterious religious configuration of giant stones in Great Britain (see Fig. 9.1). The ancient Greeks refined this system to high elegance; the most familiar of their post-and-lintel creations is the Parthenon (see Fig. 9.2).

The Greek refinement of post-and-lintel structure forms a *prototype* for buildings throughout the world and across the centuries. Therefore, it makes sense to pause to examine the Greek style in more detail. One of the more interesting aspects of the style consists of its treatment of columns and *capitals.*

Figure 9.1   *Stonehenge, Salisbury Plain, England (c. 1800–1400 B.C.E.).*
Source: Tim Draper © Rough Guides.

A Question of Style

Classical

classical (KLAS-ih-kuhl). Adhering to traditional standards. May refer to a style in art and architecture dating to the mid-fifth century B.C.E. in Athens, Greece, or ancient Rome, or any art that emphasizes simplicity, harmony, restraint, proportion, and reason. In Greek classical architecture, Doric and Ionic orders appear in temple architecture. In vase painting, geometry remains from the archaic style, but figures have a sense of idealism and lifelikeness.

The prototype of all classical buildings is the Parthenon (Fig. 9.2). The Parthenon exemplifies Greek classical architecture. Balance results from geometric symmetry, and the clean, simple lines represent a perfect balance of forces holding the composition together. In plan, the Parthenon has short sides slightly less than half the length of the long sides. The temple has peripteral form (surrounded by a single row of columns).

(*Continued*)

A Question of Style (continued)

Figure 9.2   *The Parthenon, Acropolis, Athens (448–432 B.C.E.).*
Source: © DEA/G Nimatallah/AGE Fotostock.

A specific convention determined the number of columns across the front and along the sides of the temple. The harmony of the design rests in the regular repetition of virtually unvaried forms. All the columns appear to be alike and spaced equidistantly. At the corners, however, the spacing adjusts to give a sense of grace and perfect balance, while preventing the monotony of unvaried repetition. There are, however, some refinements—that is, intentional departures from strict geometric regularity. The slight bulge of the horizontal elements compensates for the eye's tendency to see a downward sagging when all elements are straight and parallel. Each column swells toward the middle by about 7 inches to compensate for the tendency of parallel vertical lines to appear to curve inward. We call this swelling *entasis*. The columns also tilt inward slightly at the top, in order to appear perpendicular. The stylobate, or foundation, rises toward the center so as not to appear to sag under the immense weight of the stone columns and roof.

A Question of Style (continued)

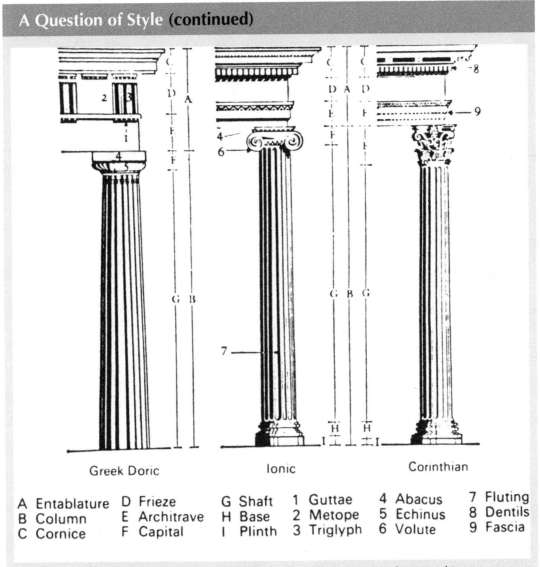

Greek Doric   Ionic   Corinthian

A Entablature D Frieze   G Shaft   1 Guttae   4 Abacus   7 Fluting
B Column   E Architrave   H Base   2 Metope   5 Echinus   8 Dentils
C Cornice   F Capital   I Plinth 3 Triglyph 6 Volute   9 Fascia

Figure 9.3   *Greek columns and capitals: (left) Doric, (center) Ionic, (right) Corinthian.*
Source: Laurence King Publishing Ltd.

Figure 9.3 shows the three basic Greek orders: Ionic, Doric, and Corinthian. These, of course, represent only some of the styles of post-and-lintel structure. Column capitals can vary as much as the imagination of the architect who designed them. They function primarily as a transition for the eye as it moves from post to lintel. Columns also may express a variety of detail—for example, *fluting*, which means vertical ridges cut into the column.

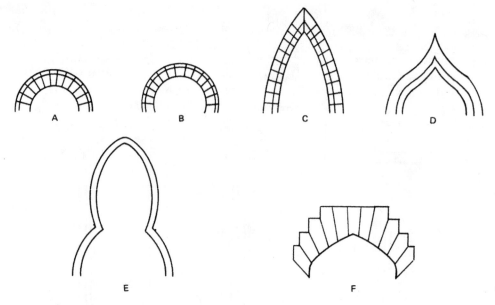

Figure 9.4   *The Arch. **A**. Round (Roman) arch. **B**. Horseshoe (Moorish) arch. **C**. Lancet (pointed, Gothic) arch. **D**. Ogee arch. **E**. Trefoil arch. **F**. Tudor arch.*

Arch

The arch represents a second type of architectural structure. As we indicated earlier, post-and-lintel structure has limitations in the amount of unencumbered space it can achieve. The arch, in contrast, can define large spaces because its stresses transfer outward from its center (the *keystone*) to its legs. Therefore, it does not depend on the tensile strength of its material.

Many different styles of arches exist, as illustrated in Figure 9.4. The characteristics of different arches may have structural as well as decorative functions.

The transfer of stress from the center of an arch outward to its legs dictates the need for a strong support to keep the legs from caving outward. Such a reinforcement is called a *buttress* (Fig. 9.5). The designers of

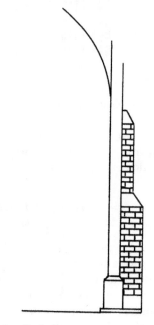

Figure 9.5   *Buttress.*

Gothic cathedrals sought to achieve a sense of lightness. Because stone formed their basic building material, they recognized some system had to be developed that would overcome the bulk of a stone buttress. Therefore, they developed a system of buttresses that accomplished structural ends but were light in appearance. These structures are called *flying buttresses* (Fig. 9.6).

Several arches placed side by side form an *arcade* (Fig. 9.7). Arches placed back to back to enclose space form a *tunnel vault* (Fig. 9.8). When two tunnel vaults intersect at right angles, as they do in the floor plan of the traditional Christian cathedral, they form a *groin vault* (Fig. 9.9). The protruding masonry indicating diagonal juncture of arches in a tunnel vault or the juncture of a groin vault is *rib vaulting* (Fig. 9.10).

When arches join at the top with their legs forming a circle, they result in a *dome*

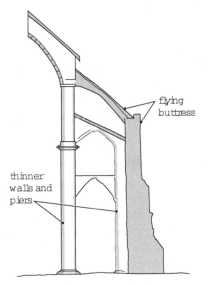

flying buttress

thinner walls and piers

Figure 9.6   *Flying buttresses.*

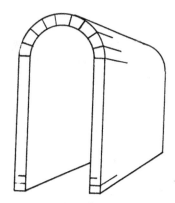

Figure 9.8   *Tunnel vault.*

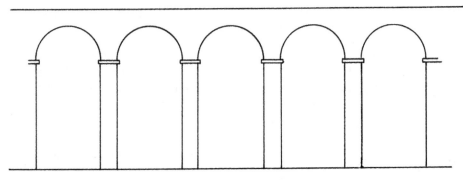

Figure 9.7   *Arcade.*

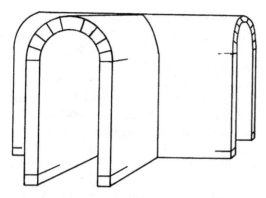

Figure 9.9   *Groin vault.*

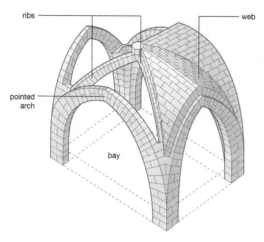

Figure 9.10   *Ribbed vault.*

such as the Dome of the Rock (see Fig. 9.11). The dome, through its intersecting arches, allows for more expansive, freer space within the structure. However, if the structures supporting the dome form a circle, they result in a circular building. To permit squared space beneath a dome, the architect can transfer weight and stress through the use of *pendentives* (see Fig. 9.12).

Cantilever

A *cantilever* comprises an overhanging beam or floor supported only at one end (see Fig. 9.13). Although not a twentieth-century innovation—many nineteenth-century barns in the central and eastern parts of the United States employed it—the most dramatic uses of cantilever have emerged with the introduction of modern materials such as steel beams and prestressed concrete (see Fig. 9.15).

Bearing-Wall

In the bearing-wall system, the wall supports itself, the floors, and the roof. Log cabins examplify bearing-wall construction; so do solid masonry buildings, in which the walls are the structure. In variations of bearing-wall construction, such as in the Church of the Holy Family (see Fig. 9.27), the wall material is continuous, that is, not jointed or pieced together. We call this variation *monolithic* construction.

Skeleton Frame

In a skeleton frame, a framework supports the building; the walls attach to the frame forming an exterior skin. When skeleton framing utilizes wood, as in house construction, we call the technique *balloon construction*. When metal forms the frame, as in skyscrapers, we call the technique *steel cage construction* (see Fig. 9.14).

BUILDING MATERIALS

Historic and contemporary architectural practices and traditions often center on specific materials, and to understand architecture further, we need to note a few.

Stone

The use of stone as a material turns us back to post-and-lintel systems and Figures 9.1 and 9.2. When stone combines with mortar,

Figure 9.11   *The Dome of the Rock mosque, known in Arabic as Al Quds (The Holy), with its golden dome on the noble Rock, Jerusalem, Israel.*
Source: Charles Bowman/Alamy Images.

for example, in arch construction, that combination results in *masonry* construction. The most obvious example of masonry, however, remains the brick wall, and masonry construction is based on that principle. Stones, bricks, or blocks are joined together with mortar, one on top of the other, to provide basic, structural, weight-bearing walls of a building, a bridge, and so forth (see Fig. 9.16). Masonry has limits because of the pressures that play on the joints between blocks and mortar and the foundation on which they rest. Great possibilities exist with this elemental combination of stone and mortar.

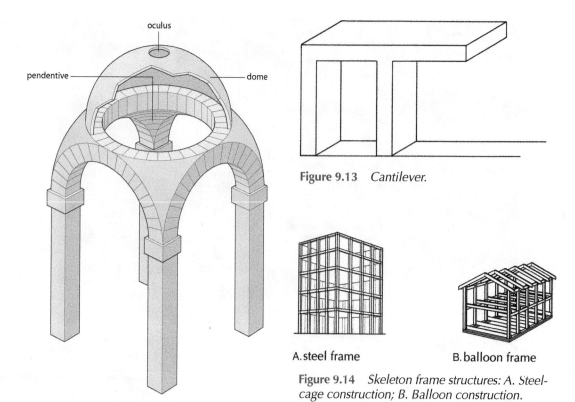

dome on pendentives
Figure 9.12   *Dome with pendentives (P).*

Figure 9.13   *Cantilever.*

A. **steel frame**   B. **balloon frame**

Figure 9.14   *Skeleton frame structures: A. Steel-cage construction; B. Balloon construction.*

Concrete

The use of concrete remains central to much contemporary architectural practice, owing its significance to as far back in the past as ancient Rome. In contemporary architecture, we find *precast* concrete (concrete cast in place using wooden forms around a steel framework). We also find *ferro-concrete* or *reinforced concrete*, which utilizes metal reinforcing embedded in the concrete. Such a technique combines the tensile strength of the metal with the compressive strength of the concrete. *Prestressed* and *posttensioned* concrete use metal rods and wires under stress or tension to cause structural forces to flow in predetermined directions. Both comprise extremely versatile building materials.

A Question to Ask

What system forms the structure of this building? Is that structure expressed outwardly or hidden?

Figure 9.15   *Grandstand, Zarzuela Race Track, Madrid (1935). Architect: Eduardo Torroja.*

Wood

Whether in balloon framing or in laminated beaming, wood has played a pivotal role, especially in the United States. As new technologies emerge in making engineered beams from what once was scrap wood, wood's continuation as a viable building product will probably remain—with less negative impact on the environment.

Steel

The use of steel comprises nearly endless variation and almost limitless possibilities for construction. Its introduction into the nineteenth-century industrial age forever changed style and scale in architecture. We noted *steel cage* construction and cantilever construction earlier. *Suspension* construction in bridges, superdomes, aerial walkways, and so on, has carried architects to the limits of space spansion. The *geodesic dome* (see Fig. 9.17) is a unique use of materials invented by an American architect, R. Buckminster Fuller (1895–1983). Consisting of a network of metal rods and hexagonal plates, the dome is a light, inexpensive, yet strong and easily assembled building. Although it has no apparent size limit (Fuller claimed he could roof New York City, given the funds), its potential for variation and aesthetic expressiveness seems somewhat limited.

Figure 9.16 *Great Enclosure, Great Zimbabwe, c. 1350–1450. Stone.*
Source: I Vanderharst/Robert Harding World Imagery.

LINE, REPETITION, AND BALANCE

Line and repetition perform the same compositional functions in architecture as in painting and sculpture. In his Kaufman House (see Fig. 9.23), Frank Lloyd Wright takes a single motif, the rectangle, varies only its size, and repeats it almost endlessly. The result, rather than being monotonous, is dynamic and fascinating.

Christopher Wren (1632–1723) designed one of the facades of Hampton Court Palace outside of London, England (see Fig. 9.18), in the classically oriented style of the English Baroque. Wren's use of line, repetition, and balance results in a sophisticated visual design and engaging perceptual experience.

As we can see, Wren designed a sophisticated and overlapping system of repetition and balance. Note first that the facade is symmetrical. The outward wing at the far right of the photograph duplicates at the left. In the center of the building reside four attached columns surrounding three windows. The middle window forms the exact center of the design, with mirror-image repetition on each side. Now note that above the main windows is a series of relief sculptures, pediments (triangular casings), and circular windows. Now

Figure 9.17 *Greenhouse domes, Mitchell Park Horticultural Conservatory, Milwaukee, Wisconsin.*
Source: Henryk Sadura/Shutterstock.

Figure 9.18 *Hampton Court Palace, England. Wren façade (1689).*
Source: John Miller/Robert Harding World Imagery.

PROFILE

Frank Lloyd Wright

Frank Lloyd Wright (1867–1959) pioneered ideas in architecture far ahead of his time and became probably the most influential architect of the twentieth century. Born in Richland Center, Wisconsin, Wright grew up under strong influences of his clergyman father's love of Bach and Beethoven. He entered the University of Wisconsin at age fifteen, forced to study engineering because the school had no program in architecture.

In 1887, Wright took a job as a draughtsman in Chicago and, the next year, joined the firm of Adler and Sullivan. In short order, Wright became Louis Sullivan's chief assistant. As Sullivan's assistant, Wright handled most of the firm's designing of houses. Deep in debt, Wright moonlighted by designing for private clients on his own. When Sullivan objected, Wright left the firm to set up his own private practice.

As an independent architect, Wright led the way in a style of architecture called the Prairie school. Houses designed in this style have low-pitched roofs and strong horizontal lines reflecting the flat landscape of the American prairie. These houses also reflect Wright's philosophy that interior and exterior spaces blend together.

In 1904, Wright designed the strong, functional Larkin Building in Buffalo, New York, and in 1906, the Unity Temple in Oak Park, Illinois. Traveling to Japan and Europe, he returned in 1911 to build a house on his grandfather's farm, Taliesin, which is Welsh for "shining brow." In 1916, Wright designed the Imperial Hotel in Tokyo, floating the structure on an underlying sea of mud. As a consequence, when the catastrophic earthquake of 1923 occurred, the hotel suffered very little damage.

The Great Depression of the 1930s greatly curtailed new building projects, and Wright spent his time writing and lecturing. In 1932, he established the Taliesin (ta-lee-AY-zihn) Fellowship, a school in which students learned by working with building materials and problems of design and construction. In winter, the school moved from Wisconsin to Taliesin West, a desert camp near Phoenix, Arizona.

The mid-1930s represented a period of intense creative output for Frank Lloyd Wright, and some of his most famous designs occurred during those years. Perhaps his most dramatic project, the Kaufman House—Falling Water—in Bear Run, Pennsylvania (see Fig. 9.23) emerged in 1936–1937 during this period. Another famous project was the S. C. Johnson and Son Administration Building in Racine, Wisconsin. The Solomon R. Guggenheim Museum (see Fig. 9.30) began in 1942 with completion in 1959.

Wright's work was always controversial, and he lived a flamboyant life full of personal tragedy and financial difficulty. Married three times, he had seven children and died in Phoenix, Arizona, on April 9, 1959.

A Question of Style

Modernism

modernism (MAH-duhr-nihz-uhm). In the arts, modernism developed as a wide-ranging reaction to romanticism and realism. It rejected conventional narrative content and conventional modes of expression to depict a world seen as altogether new and constantly in flux. In architecture, it refers to a twentieth-century style characterized by the glass and steel rectangular skyscraper (also called International Style) but with a variety of explorations of space and line including curvilinear treatments and highly symbolic exploration of form. In visual art, it includes a variety of approaches following the introduction of cubism and other "modernist" works at the International Exhibition of Modern Art (called the Armory Show) in 1913. In dance, it characterizes the nonballet tradition emphasizing angularity and asymmetry. We often associate modernism in architecture with the rectangular glass and steel box skyscraper. Modernism, however, also embraced the simple clean lines of the horizontal as well, and we can see this in Frank Lloyd Wright's Kaufman House (see Fig. 9.23). Seeming to emerge as one piece with its environment (context), the organic feeling of the building reflects Wright's belief that buildings should relate to their setting. Wright's "Falling Water," as, indeed, all his buildings, seem to grow out of, and never violate, their environment.

return to the main row of windows at the left border of the photo and count toward the center. The outer wing contains four windows; then seven windows; then the central three; then seven; and finally the four of the outer wing. Patterns of threes and sevens are very popular in architecture and carry religious and mythological symbolism. Wren established a pattern of four in the outer wing, three in the center, and then repeated it within each of the seven-window groups to create yet three additional patterns of three! How can he create four patterns of three with only seven windows? First, locate the center window of the seven. It has a pediment and a relief sculpture above it. On each side of this window are three windows (a total of six) without pediments. So, we have *two* groupings of three windows each. Above each of the outside four windows is a circular window. The window on each side of the center window does not have

a circular window above it. Rather, it has a relief sculpture, the presence of which joins these two windows with the center window to give us our third grouping of three. Line, repetition, and balance in this facade form a marvelous perceptual exercise and experience.

Byodo-in (by-oh-doh-ihn; Fig. 9.19) and the Palace of Versailles (Fig. 9.20) have similar compositional geometry in a central pavilion, symmetrical side wings, and projecting porticos anchoring the ends of the buildings. Through differing use of line, however, they achieve widely different visual results. Curved roof lines in the Byodo-in sweep the eye upward, and the thin pillars of contrasting straight character seem to lift the building from its foundations. Juxtaposing simple curved and straight lines in this fashion varies significantly from the play of curved against straight in a more ornate way in the Palace of Versailles, in which repetition occurs in groupings of threes

Figure 9.19 *Byodo-in, Uji, Kyoto prefecture, Japan. Heian period, c. 1053 C.E.*
Source: © Catherine Karnow/Corbis.

Figure 9.20 *Palace of Versailles, France (1669–1685). Architects: Louis LeVau and Jules Hardouin-Mansart.*
Source: Werner Otto/Robert Harding World Imagery.

and fives and contrast occurs by juxtaposition and repetition of curved lines in the arched windows and Baroque statuary. Notice how the horizontal shape of the building, despite three porticos, remains virtually undisturbed, in contrast with that of Byodo-in.

SCALE AND PROPORTION

Scale in architecture refers to a building's size and the relationship of the building and its decorative elements to the human form. Proportion, or the relationship of individual elements to each other, also plays an important role in a building's visual effect. Scale may range from an intimate bungalow, for example, to the towering power of a skyscraper (see Fig. 9.33). Proportion and scale are tools with which the architect can create relationships that may be straightforward or deceptive. We must decide how these elements are used and to what effect. In addition, proportion in many buildings is mathematical: The relationships of one part to another often form ratios of three to two, one to two, one to three, and so on. Discovering such relationships in a building challenges us whenever we encounter a work of architecture.

CONTEXT

An architectural design must take into account its context, or environment. In many cases, context is essential to the statement made by the design or shapes the design itself, as in the case of the Anasazi cliff dwellings shown in Figure 9.21. The cathedral of Notre Dame, Chartres (Fig. 9.22) sits

Figure 9.21 *Cliff architecture, Anasazi Culture, Mesa Verde, Colorado, c. 1100–1200. Adobe.*
Source: George H. H. Huey/Corbis.

Figure 9.22   *Exterior, Cathedral of Notre Dame, Chartres, France (1145–1220).*
Source: Herve Champollion/Caisse Nationale des Monuments Historique et des Sites, Paris, France.

at the center of, and on the highest point in, the village of Chartres, France. Its placement at that particular location had a purpose for the medieval artisans and clerics responsible for its design. The centrality of the cathedral to the community made an essential statement of the centrality of the Church to the life of the medieval community. Context also has a psychological bearing on scale. A skyscraper in the midst of skyscrapers has great mass but does not appear as massive in scale when overshadowed by another, taller skyscraper. A cathedral, when compared with a skyscraper, appears relatively small in scale. However, when standing at the center of a community of small houses, it seems quite the opposite.

Two additional aspects of context concern the design of line, form, and texture relative to the physical environment of the building. On one hand, the environment can be shaped according to the compositional qualities of the building. Perhaps the best illustration of that principle is Louis XIV's palace at Versailles (Fig. 9.20), whose formal symmetry is reflected in the design of thousands of acres around it.

In contrast, a building may be designed to reflect the natural characteristics of its environment. Frank Lloyd Wright's "Falling Water" (Fig. 9.23) illustrates this principle. Such an idea has been advanced by many architects and can be seen especially in residences in which large expanses of glass allow

Figure 9.23 *Frank Lloyd Wright (1867–1959), Kaufman House, "Falling Water," Bear Run, Pennsylvania, 1936–1937.*
Source: Jan Moline/Photo Researchers, Inc.

A Question to Ask

In what ways does the building reflect or compete with its context?

us to feel a part of the outside while we are inside. The interior decoration of such houses often takes as its theme the colors, textures, lines, and forms of the environment surrounding the home. Natural fibers, earth tones, delicate wooden furniture, pictures that reflect the surroundings, large open spaces—together they form the core of the design, selection, and placement of nearly every item in the home, from walls to furniture to silverware. Sometimes a building seems at odds with its context. Situated in the middle of historic Paris near the old marketplace, Les Halles, the Pompidou Centre (Fig. 9.24), an art museum whose brightly painted infrastructure appears on the outside of the building, seems out of place beside its more ancient neighbors.

SPACE

It seems almost absurdly logical to state that architecture must concern space—for what else, by definition, is architecture?

Figure 9.24 *Renzo Piano and Richard Rogers, Centre Pompidou, Paris, opened 1977.*
Source: © Iain Masterton/age fotostock.

However, the world teems with examples of architectural design that have not met that need. Design of space essentially means the design and flow of contiguous *spaces* relative to function. Take, for example, a sports arena. Of primary concern is the space necessary for the sports intended to occupy the building. Will it play host to basketball, hockey, track, football, or baseball? Each of these sports places a design restriction on the architect, and curious results occur when functions not intended by the design force themselves into its parameters. When the Brooklyn Dodgers moved to Los Angeles, they played for a time in the Los Angeles Coliseum, a facility designed for the Olympic games and track and field and reasonably suited for the addition of football. However, the imposition of baseball created ridiculous effects; the left-field fence was only slightly over 200 feet from home plate.

In addition to the requirements of the game, a sports arena must also accommodate the requirements of the spectators. Pillars that obstruct the spectator's view do not create goodwill and the purchase of tickets. Likewise, attempting to put more seats in a confined space than ought to be there can create great discomfort. Determining where to draw the line between more seats and fan comfort is not easy.

Further, we can see the design of space in a monumental work of landscape architecture, New York's Central Park (Fig. 9.25). Here the use of space incorporates formal elements such as tree-lined malls and classical fountains as well as informal elements

A Question of Style

Postmodern

postmodern (pohst-MAHD-uhrn). In visual art, architecture, dance, and literature, a diverse, highly individualistic style that rejects modernism and its principles. It is distinguished by eclecticism and anachronism, in which works may reflect and comment on a wide range of stylistic expressions and cultural–historical viewpoints, including breaking down the distinctions between "high art" and popular culture. Self-reference is often at the center of creation and presentation. One common theme appears to be a basic concern for how art functions in society. In architecture, it seeks social identity, cultural continuity, and sense of place. We see the tenets of postmodernism and its repudiation of the glass-and-steel box of the modern, International, style in the design of the Pompidou (pohm-pee-DOO) Center in Paris (Fig. 9.24). The building literally turns inside out, with its network of ducts, pipes, and elevators color-coded and externalized, and its internal structure hidden. The interior spaces have no fixed walls, but temporary dividers allow any configuration wanted. The bright primary colors on the exterior combine with the serpentine, Plexiglas-covered escalators to give a whimsical, lively appearance to a functional building. The Pompidou Center has become a tourist attraction in Paris rivaling the Eiffel Tower, and, while controversial, it has gained wide popular acceptance.

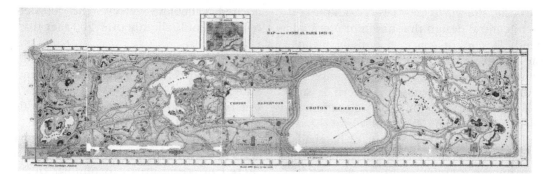

Figure 9.25   *Frederick Law Olmsted and Calvert Vaux, Map of Central Park, New York City, 1858–1880. Revised and extended park layout as shown in a map of 1873.*
The rectangular water tanks in the middle of the park were later removed and replaced by a large, elliptical meadow known as the Great Lawn.
Source: City of New York, Department of Parks.

including naturalism in topographical irregularities and plantings, natural rock outcroppings, and asymmetrical trails and walking paths.

CLIMATE

Climate always has been a factor in architectural design in zones of severe temperature, either hot or cold. As the world's energy supplies diminish, this factor will grow in importance. In the temperate climate of much of the United States, solar systems and designs that make use of the moderating influence of the Earth are common. These are *passive* systems—that is, their design accommodates natural phenomena rather than adding technological devices such as solar collectors. For example, in the colder sections of the United States a building can be made energy efficient by being designed with no glass, or minimal glass, on its north-facing side. Windows facing south can be covered or uncovered to catch existing sunlight, which even in midwinter provides considerable warmth. Also, because temperatures at the shallow depth of 3 feet below Earth's surface rarely exceed or go below 50 degrees regardless of season, Earth presents a gold mine of potential for design. Houses built into the sides of hills or recessed below Earth's surface require much less heating or cooling than those standing fully exposed—regardless of climate extremes. Even in zones of uniform and moderate temperature, climate is a design factor. The "California lifestyle," as it often is known, has created design that accommodates easy access to the out-of-doors, and large, open spaces with free-flowing traffic patterns.

A Question to Ask

How does the building either assist or inhibit a smooth traffic flow through its spaces?

HOW DOES IT STIMULATE THE SENSES?

As should be clear at this point, our sensual response to a form of aesthetic design consists of a composite experience. To be sure, the individual characteristics we have discussed previously stimulate our response. Lately, color has become an important tool to the postmodern architect in stimulating our sense responses. The effects of color in the Pompidou Centre (see Fig. 9.24) turn architecture into an exotic sensual experience.

CONTROLLED VISION AND SYMBOLISM

The Gothic cathedral has been described as the perfect synthesis of intellect, spirituality, and engineering. The upward, striving line of the Gothic arch makes a simple yet powerful statement of medieval people's striving to understand their earthly relation to the spiritual unknown. Even today the simplicity and grace of that design have an effect on most who view a Gothic cathedral. Chartres' cathedral of Notre Dame (see Figs. 9.22 and 9.26), unlike the symmetry of other gothic churches, has an asymmetrical design, arising from the replacement of one of its steeples because of fire. The new steeple reflects a later and more complex Gothic style, and as a result impedes the eye as it progresses upward. Only after some pause does the eye reach the tip of the spire, the point of which symbolizes the individual's escape from the earthly known to the unknown.

Included in this grandeur of simple vertical line is an ethereal lightness that defies the material from which the cathedral is constructed. The medieval architect has

Figure 9.26   *Interior, Cathedral of Notre Dame, Chartres, France (1145–1220).*
Source: John Parker © Dorling Kindersley.

created in stone not the heavy yet elegant composition of the early Greeks, which focused on treatment of stone, but rather a treatment of stone that focuses on space—the ultimate mystery. Inside the cathedral the design of stained glass kept high above the worshipers' heads controls the light entering the cathedral to effect an overwhelming sense of mystery. Line, form, scale, color, structure, balance, proportion, context, and space all combine to form a unified composition that has stood for nearly eight hundred years as a prototype and symbol of the Christian experience.

STYLE

The Christian experience forms the denominator of the design of the Church of the Holy Family (Fig. 9.27). However, despite the clarity of line and the upward striving power of its composition, this church suggests modern sophistication through its style, perhaps speaking more of our own conception of space, which to us seems less unknowable and more conquerable, than it seemed to our medieval predecessors. The juxtaposing of rectilinear and curvilinear line creates an active and dynamic response, one that prompts in us abruptness rather than

mystery. The composition evolves coolness, and its material calls attention to itself—to its starkness and to its lack of decoration.

Each part of the church emerges distinctly and does not quite subordinate to the totality of the design. This building perhaps represents a philosophy intermediate between the philosophy underlying the Cathedral of Notre Dame, whose entire design can be reduced to a single motif—the Gothic arch—and the philosophy such as the baroque style, as seen in the Hall of Mirrors of the Palace of Versailles (see Fig. 9.28). No single part of the design of this hall epitomizes the whole, yet each part is subordinate to the

Figure 9.27   *The Church of the Holy Family, Parma, Ohio (1965). Architects: Conrad and Fleishman.*

Figure 9.28 *Hall of Mirrors, Palace of Versailles, France (1680). Architects: Jules Hardouin-Mansart and Charles LeBrun.*
Courtesy of Jose Igancio Soto/Shutterstock.

whole. Our response to the hall is shaped by its ornate complexity, which calls for detachment and investigation and intends to overwhelm us with its opulence. Here, as in most art, the expression and the stimuli reflect the patron. The Cathedral of Notre Dame reflects the medieval church, the Church of the Holy Family, the contemporary church, and Versailles, the absolute monarchy of King Louis XIV. Versailles is complex, highly active, and yet warm. The richness of its textures, the warmth of its colors, and its curvilinear softness create

Figure 9.29   *United States Capitol Building (1792–1856). Washington, D.C.*
Source: James Pickerell/The Image Works.

a certain kind of comfort despite its scale and formality.

In the U.S. Capitol, a neoclassic house of government (Fig. 9.29), formality creates a foursquare, solid response. The symmetry of its design, the weight of its material, and its coldness give us a sense of impersonal power, which is heightened by the crushing weight of the dome. Rather than the upward-striving spiritual release of the Gothic arch, or even the powerful elegance of the Greek post-and-lintel, the Capitol building, based on Michelangelo's design for St. Peter's Basilica, Rome, elicits a sense of struggle. This is achieved through upward columnar thrust (heightened by the context provided by Capitol Hill) and downward thrust (of the dome) focused toward the interior of the building.

APPARENT FUNCTION

The architect Louis Sullivan, of whom Frank Lloyd Wright was a pupil, is credited with the concept that form follows function. To a degree, we have seen that concept in the previous examples, even though, with the exception of the Church of the Holy Family, they all precede Sullivan in time. A worthy question concerning the Guggenheim Museum (see Fig. 9.30) might be how well Wright followed his teacher's philosophy. There is a story that Wright hated New York City because of

Figure 9.30 *The Solomon R. Guggenheim Museum, New York City (1942–1959). Architect: Frank Lloyd Wright.* Source: Dave King © Dorling Kindersley.

unpleasant experiences he had had with the city fathers during previous projects. As a result, the Guggenheim, done late in his life, became his final gesture of derision to the city. This center of contemporary culture and art, with its single, circular ramp from street level to roof, was built (so the story goes) from the plans for a parking garage. Be that as it may, the line and form of this building create a simple, smoothly flowing, leisurely, upward movement juxtaposed against a stark and dynamic rectilinear form. The building's line and color and the feeling they produce are contemporary statements appropriate to the contemporary art the museum houses. The modern design of the Guggenheim contrasts with the classical proportions of the Metropolitan Museum of Art, just down the street, which houses great works of ancient and modern art. The interior design is outwardly expressed in the ramp, and one can speculate that the slowly curving, unbroken line of the ramp is highly appropriate to the leisurely pace that one should follow when going through a museum.

DYNAMICS

Leisurely progress through the Guggenheim diametrically opposes the sensation stimulated by the cantilevered roof of the grandstand at Zarzuela Race Track in Spain (see Fig. 9.15). Speed, power, and flight are its preeminent concerns. The sense of dynamic instability inherent in the structural form—that is, cantilever, and this particular application of that form—mirror the dynamic instability and forward power of the race horse at full speed. However, despite the form and the strong diagonals of this design, it is not out of control; the architect has unified the design through repetition of the track-level arcade in the arched line of the cantilevered roof. The design is dynamic and yet humanized in the softness of its curves and the control of its scale.

Dynamics also defines Canadian-born architect Frank Gehry's (GHAIR-ee; b. 1929) Disney Hall in Los Angeles, California (Fig. 9.31). His architectural theory creates functional works of sculpture rather than

Figure 9.31   *Frank Gehry, Walt Disney Concert Hall, Los Angeles, California (opened 2003).*
Source: Photononstop/Superstock/Art Life Images.

buildings in the traditional sense. His early works witnessed an architectural language of plywood and corrugated metal. Later, these evolved into distorted but lucid concrete and metal. They reflect an aesthetic that appears somewhat disjointed, as if attempting to belong to social context likewise disjointed. Disney Hall in Los Angeles, California, suggests to some the sails of a ship. It also can suggest the turmoil of our times in its "visual chaos." This building, along with Gehry's Guggenheim Museum building in Bilbao, Spain, attempts to change the language of architecture. Both stand like immense works of sculpture against the background of the city and continue a curvaceous, free-form style that has become the architect's signature. He utilized similar abstract, free-form

A Question to Ask

In what ways do the dynamics of the building stimulate an emotional or intellectual response in me? Why is this so?

Figure 9.32   *Diller Scofidio + Renfro, Blur Building, Yverdon-les-Bains, Switzerland, 2002.*
Source: Diller Scofidio + Renfro.

components in other works such as the Gehry House and the Fishdance Restaurant, which employ a similarly sleek curvaceous cladding. The forms of the building take on sculptured dimensions so complex that they required an advanced aerospace computer program to allow the contractor to build the building in a reasonable way.

Elizabeth Diller (b. 1955) and Ricardo Scofidio (b. 1942) together form Diller Scofidio + Renfro, a collaborative interdisciplinary studio involved in architecture, the visual arts, and the performing arts. Their Blur Building, a media building for Swiss EXPO 2002, turns architecture into performance art. Blur Building (Fig. 9.32) constitutes a cloud measuring 300 feet wide by 200 feet deep hovering over Lake Nuechâtel in Yverdon-les-Bains, Switzerland, and floating at a height of 75 feet above the water. The cloud consists of filtered lake water shot as a fine mist through a dense array of high-pressure fog nozzles. The artificial cloud creates a dynamic form that constantly changes shape in response to actual weather: A built-in weather station electronically adjusts the water pressure and temperature in thirteen zones according to shifting humidity, wind direction, and speed.

The public can approach the cloud from shore via pedestrian ramp. Upon entering, the visitor finds visual and acoustical references slowly erased, leaving only an optical "white-out" and the "white noise" of pulsing fog nozzles. Sensory deprivation stimulates a sensory heightening: The density of air inhaled with every breath, the lowered temperature, the soft sound of water spray, and the scent of atomized water begin to overwhelm the senses. The public can circulate through the cloud, enter an interactive media space at its center, discover small media events distributed just outside in the fog, then proceed up and emerge, in the words of the architects, "like an airplane piercing a cloud layer" to the Angel Bar at the summit.

SCALE

Nothing suggests the technological achievement of modern humans more than the overwhelming scale of the skyscraper. Also, nothing symbolizes the subordination of humans to their technology like the scale of the Burj Khalifa (2010; Fig. 9.33), the tallest building in the world in all four categories as recognized by the Council on Tall Buildings and Urban Habitat, having the highest publicly accessible observation deck, and the world's fastest lift, which will shoot along at 65 km/hour (40 mph). Designed by the architects Skidmore, Owings, and Merrill, the Burj Khalifa, in Dubai, United Arab Emirates, will have 200 floors and cost $800 million. As a point of departure, its appeal to our senses raises the question of what comes next, the conquest of space or a return to respect for its natural mysteries?

Figure 9.33 *Skidmore, Owings, & Merrill, Burj Khalifa, Dubai, United Arab Emirates (2009).*
Source: KENCKOphotography/Shutterstock.

Figure 9.34   *Zaha Hadid, Lois and Richard Rosenthal Center for Contemporary Art, Cincinnati, Ohio, opened 2003.*
Source: © Arcaid/Alamy.

Sample Outline and Critical Analysis

The following very brief example illustrates how we can use our own personal response as a starting point along with some of the terms explained in the chapter to form an outline and then develop a critical analysis of a work of art. Here is how that might work regarding Baghdad-born and London-based architect Zaha Hadid's Lois and Richard Rosenthal Center for Contemporary Art in Cincinnati, Ohio (Fig. 9.34).

Outline	Critical Analysis
Personal reaction	An inventory of initial personal reactions to the museum includes sensations like dynamism, warmth, and friendliness, and these play off other sensations like awkwardness, cramping, and edginess. Fundamentally, I like looking at the building. It has a terrific sense of movement caused by its almost inverted pyramidal design; that is, the top is wider than the bottom. That, however, is where the awkwardness comes in. It feels like the building defies gravity and might tip over at any minute. All the jutting angles and pure rectilinear forms seem edgy and sharp without much sense of softness, but at the same time, the building seems warm, open, people friendly, and human in scale.
Structure	The specific structure of the building remains hidden, but the openness of the first, third, and fourth floors suggest steel cage.
Materials	Knowing that the edifice is an art museum suggests the need for large, open areas, meaning that the walls probably are curtain walls hanging from the skeleton. She has effectively employed cantilever, which gives the building most of its dynamism. The architect has used a variety of materials: glass, steel, concrete, and perhaps other materials in the decorative rectangles appended to the front and side of the building.
Context	The building seems squeezed into its context, sandwiched among larger buildings that tower over it in the rear, and similar-sized buildings that partner it along the street to its left. Ms. Hadid has made maximum use of the site, however, letting the building rise vertically, and yet at street level she has set the tower back from the perimeter of the site. The open space around the building creates its own envelope of environment.
Space	The extensive use of glass opens the building to view, and we see open public areas and some of the galleries, which appear to allow the free flow of movement required for viewing art in a museum context.

5 Film

Writing About Film

Writing about film shares a number of characteristics with writing about other arts, particularly writing about drama, fiction, and music. We will take up some of the similarities and differences between film and these other arts as part of our introductory discussion of the nature of film.

But just what is film, anyway? What do we mean when we refer to film? In common speech we refer to films as "movies," though we sometimes use the word "films" as well. The singular word "film" as distinguished from the plural terms "films" and "movies" (in the context of this discussion) refers to the general features and overall capacity of the medium. A third term, "cinema," is more formal and academic. It connotes the serious side of film, in which technical, theoretical, and aesthetic issues are paramount.

James Monaco* distinguishes among these terms in the following way: According to Monaco, who follows French film theorists, film concerns the relationship of film artworks with the world around them; cinema, on the other hand, refers to the aesthetic and internal structure of their art and artistry. In this schema, movies are seen as more commercial enterprises and represent their economic aspect.

Whatever terms we use to designate these varying aspects of film (and we will use this term to refer to the genre in general), it should be noted that a variety of films can be described according to function and intent. One kind of spectrum would put documentary films on one end, mass-market entertainment films in the middle, and "art" films on the other end. Another way to distinguish among films is according to film genres with categories such as historical films, westerns, horror movies, gangster

---

*This chapter is indebted to James Monaco's *How to Read a Film*, 3rd ed., New York: Oxford University Press, 2000.

films, war films, action films, fantasy and science-fiction films, romantic comedies, films based on novels, and so on.

In this chapter our concern is to consider how we might view a film, whatever its type, carefully enough to be able to write about it. Our goal is to consider some of the special qualities of films, though without entering into detailed technical questions.

FILM AND THE OTHER ARTS

Viewing a film in a movie theater shares some similarities with viewing a play in a theater designed for the enactment of drama. In both instances, we are usually seeing human actors portraying various roles of the story being dramatized. In viewing both films and plays, the audience enters their worlds with a temporary suspension of disbelief that what we are watching are real events experienced in real time by actual people. We suspend our disbelief in the artifice and in the fictional world we are viewing until the performance is over, and we applaud (or not) what we have seen.

But there are some significant differences between theater and film, between plays and movies. In most plays, there is no clearly defined point of view, as there is in film. Although playwrights can keep the focus on their characters through speech and action, filmmakers control the way we see their films through decisions about what images and scenes to film, through controlling exactly what the audience is permitted to see. A playwright cannot control where the audience looks or what it focuses on as it watches a play. On the other hand, an audience of a film sees only what the filmmaker decides to let it see.

Other differences between films and plays include the constant perspective or distance maintained between an audience and the actors dramatizing a scene in a play and the varying degrees of close-up and long-shot views a filmmaker can provide in a film. That's why stage actors work so hard to develop their voices, both to project and to convey nuances of feeling. Stage actors also need to develop bodily gesture, whereas film actors have to use facial expression more carefully and diligently, allowing for the possibilities of the camera close-up shot.

Still other differences are attributable to the technical limitations and possibilities allowed on stage and screen. Although stage and set designers have exercised great ingenuity in creating stage sets for plays, film set designers have greater latitude because of the technology available to them, particularly since the advent of digitalization.

Films also have close connections with fiction, particularly with novels. Unlike drama, films and novels are driven by their narrative impulse—their impulse to tell a story. Although films are less limited in what they can do visually than are plays, they are more limited than novels in their handling of time. While it is certainly true that plays and films can suggest shifts in time from present to past and back again, the novelist has a considerably easier task in adjusting not only such time shifts, but also the ways that time can be speeded up or stretched out, giving a few words to many years or many pages, even an entire volume, to a single day, as James Joyce does in *Ulysses*.

Like plays, too, films are subject to the attention span of their audiences, while readers can pick up and put down novels, since they are not limited by the duration of a film or a theatrical performance. The biggest difference, of course, between novels and films and theatrical productions is the verbal/visual distinction. An audience sees actors portraying characters, on the one hand, as they are presented by filmmakers, dramatists, and directors of movies and plays. Readers, on the other hand, must imagine characters and scenes as they are created by and suggested through the medium of writing, of words on a page. Readers, in a sense, must conspire with writers to bring characters, actions, and scenes to life in ways they do not when watching a play or a film.

Like theater, film has both a pictorial and a musical dimension. Images in films are momentarily pictorial, like paintings. Of course the images move, which differentiates them from paintings. Films also include soundtracks, which typically include significant amounts of music. And just as in concert music, film music affects audiences emotionally, though concert music exists in and takes its meaning from itself, whereas film music exists as part of a larger and predominantly visual and narrative art.

We might identify still other ways in which film is similar to and different from the other arts, but these comparative and contrastive elements can help us consider the special nature and quality of film en route to reading and writing about films.

READING A FILM

In "reading" a film, we interpret it, attempting to understand its implications, to make sense of it. When reading a film, we ask ourselves what its producer and director intended its audience to experience and understand through viewing it.

In learning to read films, we can consider some of the same elements that we considered in discussing reading fiction and drama—plot and structure, character and conflict, point of view, staging and setting—as well as aspects such as irony and symbolism. In writing about films, you may wish to focus on such elements or aspects; you can consult the discussion of those elements in Chapters 5 and 6. Here, however, we briefly discuss a few elements special to film, although some of them have counterparts in the other arts.

ELEMENTS OF FILM

Just as we refer to the elements of literature, drama, and the other arts, we can also approach film through a consideration of its special features. Among those we consider here are photography, acting, *mise en scene* and movement, editing, sound and music.

Photography (Shots)

Although the smallest element of film is the single image, filmmakers work with shots and sequences of shots to create a scene or a sequence of scenes. The film shots are typically taken at different times—often involving repeated takes to create a scene. Scenes themselves are usually edited later with shots from the different takes, so that what an audience sees has been constructed from many takes of individual shots and scenes to construct the finished sequences that constitute the completed film.

Films may be shot primarily in close-ups, which tend to be disorienting because we don't see background and context. On the other hand, films may be made primarily with long shots, which tend to emphasize context and action and to downplay character and personality. Most films, of course, combine these two very different shot styles and incorporate a variety of approaches to them.

One key aspect of a film shot is focus. Deep focus shots, which keep foreground, middle ground, and background all in reasonably sharp focus. Shallow focus shots allow the director to emphasize one of these, foreground, for example, over the others. The focus of a shot can also be made sharp or soft, with a sharp focus often emphasizing a realistic edge, a life-like verisimilitude, and a soft focus emphasizing a more attenuated, sometimes romanticized image.

Additional factors affecting the way film shots look to an audience are its angle of approach, lighting, and composition. Shots made from a high angle make the subject look smaller and less important, whereas shots from a low angle emphasize the size and significance, even the power of the subject. Lighting can create all sorts of effects, with characters appearing in full or partial light, backlit, and also partially lit and partially shadowed, with one character or one feature of a single character highlighted.

The sequence of shots on page 89 includes both mid-range and close-up shots.

These stills from Eisenstein's *Battleship Potemkin* reveal the director's dramatic use of close-ups and his use of contrasting mid-range shots in starkly realistic style.

Sergei Eisenstein, "Battleship Potemkin," 1925. Goskino, Courtesy of Everett Collection, Inc.

Acting

One of the first questions we often ask about a new film is who is in it, what actors are starring in the film. We may also want to know who produced and directed it, but mostly our interest centers on the actors and the roles they play in films. From the beginning, the film industry centered on its stars, a small number of actors (and actresses, when that term was in use) who had major drawing power, appealing to large audiences of viewers. Today we have Matt Damon, Tom Cruise, Jennifer Lopez, and others; in the past there were Clark Gable, Rock Hudson, Marlene Dietrich, Ava Gardner, Katherine Hepburn, Humphrey Bogart, and numerous others through the years.

Actors, however, are not all stars. Many actors serve in type-cast, familiar secondary roles; these character actors, as they are known, can become familiar screen (or television) faces, though they don't assume the role or possess the drawing power and name recognition of stars. In addition, some directors will cast nonprofessionals in acting roles in films, as did Vittoria de Sica, in his classic film *The Bicycle Thief*. Also appearing in films are "extras," the people used to fill out crowd scenes and background scenes for the stars of a film.

In viewing a film, we should attend to an actor's performance in his or her given role. We should ask ourselves how well the actor carries the role. Is the actor's performance convincing? Does the actor make you believe in the character's situation and circumstances and behavior? Some criteria you can use to analyze and evaluate an actor's performance when writing include the following:

- Is the actor well suited to the role for which he or she has been cast?
- How well did the actor's voice, gestures, and facial expressions convey the character being portrayed?
- Is the actor believable in the role? Why or why not?
- In which scenes does the actor excel—or not excel? Why?
- How well does the actor relate to the other actors and their roles in the film?

Mise en Scene and Movement

The term *mise en scene* is a French phrase that refers to theater, meaning "placing on stage." It involves the arrangement of all the visual elements on the stage of a theatrical production. With respect to film, *mise en scene* refers to the visual elements of a film, from its still shots to the patterns of changing images we see as the film's action moves in a constant flux. Just as in viewing any single image from a film, a still such as a close-up or long-distance camera shot, in viewing the moving film images, you should be alert for the visual patterns created and their effects on viewers.

We can be alert for how the director arranges the actors in a given scene and how the scenes are sequenced to create a particular design or pattern of designs. One of the most common principles for sequencing shots and scenes is contrast. Consider, for example, the way the *Star Wars* films or the *Lord of the Rings* trilogy of films handles battle scenes, alternating between long shots of vast armies with close-ups of the effect of the devastation on particular individuals. Just as we examine the composition of a painting by analyzing the orderly arrangement of its parts, so too do we with film shots. And just as we can analyze the way a play's scenes flow visually from one to another and its sets change, so too can we consider the flow and changing scenes in a film from a similar perspective—though in a film, of course, the changes are much more rapid.

Another aspect of the moving images of films is the physical movement of the actors, their kinetic dimension, and then, in addition, the ways in which actors' movements combine and commingle in shifting scenes. Think, for example, of slapstick comedy routines of characters such as Laurel and Hardy or the Three Stooges. Or think of the way physical movement plays out in films such as *Crouching Tiger, Hidden Dragon*, or the aerial acrobatics of films involving plane fights, such as those in the Tom Cruise film *Top Gun*.

Some questions to consider when analyzing and writing about the visual effects of *mise en scene* and movement are the following:

- How does the film's setting contribute to its overall emotional atmosphere?
- How is the setting related to the plot and the characters of the film?
- To what extent is the setting realistic, symbolic, fantastic?
- What kinds of repetition and contrast do you notice in the flow of scenes? What effects do the repetitions and contrasts create?
- To what extent is the film's action presented as occurring in a realistic, recognizable temporal manner, and to what extent is the action slowed down or speeded up—and with what effects?
- What is the overall impression created by the film's visual details and their arrangement?

Editing

Film editing is a highly complex and extremely important art and film element. Editing affects the look and feel as well as the rhythm and pacing of a film. The extent to which the camera lingers on a shot and scene, and the extent to which it moves slowly across a wide shot, affect the emotional as well as visual implications of a film. Lingering shots tend toward languor; fast, quick shots that jump from one to another create a kind of edginess.

Film shots are edited to create continuity in the action—or to create discontinuity and disrupted action. It depends on what effects the director is aiming for. Editing also allows films to present action realistically without having to do so in "real time." For example, in shooting a scene in which a pair of lovers walk across a bridge under lamplight, stop halfway to talk, resume their walk, and then stop again to kiss, might take a few minutes of real time to film. In the edited version, three or four shots strung together can depict that action in a matter of seconds.

One important aspect of editing is montage, sequences of rapidly edited images, often transitional, to suggest the lapse of time or the passing of events. Montage editing was a specialty of the great Russian filmmaker Sergei Eisenstein, best known for his silent film, *Battleship Potemkin*, which includes a famous montage referred to as the Odessa steps sequence or montage. Four images of that montage appear on page 103.

Some questions to keep in mind when you analyze and write about a film's editing are:

- How fast or slow are the shot sequences? How consistent are they throughout the film? With what effects?
- Does the film employ much cutting between and among scenes, or is it relatively fluid and continuous? With what effects?
- How are changes of time and place—transitions—indicated?
- What kinds of juxtapositions of scene, perhaps extending to montage, do you notice, and with what effects?

Sound and Music

Although film is primarily a visual medium, it also includes an aural component—sound, which includes, but is not limited, to the use of music. Films incorporate many kinds of sounds in many ways and for a variety of purposes. The most notable but perhaps taken for granted is the sound of speech, the film's dialogue. There may also be a narrative voice-over of an unseen speaker, who comments on the film's characters and action, and who fills in plot details, and more. Of course, there are also on- and off-screen sounds—of cars starting, glass shattering, sirens sounding, bombs exploding, for some examples of loud sounds—and for softer ones, of people breathing, lights being clicked on, matches struck, and the like. Directors—and actors—use sound effects to establish tone, enhance character revelation, and create and enhance setting, as well as to advance the film's action.

Music, the score for a film, is an important sound element. Music can be used as a background hardly noticeable; it can be used to heighten suspense, to reveal character, to intensify emotion. Much of the time when we watch a film, we hardly notice the music. But if you switch off the sound and watch in silence, you detect a difference in the character and the quality of the viewing experience, since music contributes heavily to a film's effects.

Here are a few questions to consider when analyzing and writing about a film's sound and music:

Guidelines for Analyzing Film Sound and Music

- What kinds of sounds, on or off screen, does the film include? For what purposes?
- What sound effects seem most important in the film? Why?
- To what extent does the film use sound to convey a character's state of mind? How? With what effects?

- To what extent is sound used for transitions or scene shifts in the film? With what effects?
- Does the musical score of the film remain in the background (background music), or does it assume greater prominence? Where? With what effects?
- To what extent does the music convey or create emotion? To what extent does it convey a character's thoughts and feelings?
- How would the viewing experience differ if the music, the film score, were omitted?

DOCUMENTARY FILMS

Among the many film genres is the documentary. A documentary film presents factual information about life in the world. Unlike typical feature films, which are fictional, documentary films attempt to describe the world as it is. It is important to note, however, that regardless of how factual a documentary film may be, it always expresses a particular point of view—a stance or perspective on reality. Classic documentaries such as *Nanook of the North*, about Eskimo life, approach their topic as objectively as possible, providing information. A recent example is the Academy Award winner in the documentary category, *March of the Penguins*. But this recent film, and a documentary such as *Hearts and Minds*, about the Vietnam War, attempt to do more than just provide information. These films, like many documentaries, attempt to move an audience emotionally and perhaps, as in the case of the Vietnam film, to present a political argument. Other recent documentaries expressing strong political viewpoints include those of the director, Michael Moore, especially *Sicko*, about the healthcare industry.

A documentary, then, will very likely take a stand on an issue, and perhaps offer a solution to a problem, as well as provide information. Documentary films remain based on fact, on things that have actually occurred or are really happening. However, through selection of certain details, omission of other details, selection and sequencing of scenes, documentary filmmakers convey their ideas about the world as they see it.

Some of the elements used in documentary films are newsreels, pictures from archives, interviews, and prerecorded music (sometimes archival period recordings). All these elements can be found in the highly successful documentary films—actually series of films—produced by Ken Burns, which were shown to great acclaim on public television, and which are now available on DVD. These documentary film series include *The Civil War*, *Jazz*, and *Baseball*.

Here are some questions to consider when viewing and writing about a documentary film:

- What are the purpose and point of the documentary?
- To what extent is the director's point of view about the topic evident?
- To what extent is the documentary an attempt to persuade viewers toward a specific point of view? To what degree is the documentary informational?
- What documentary elements does the film include? With what degree of success?

EXERCISES

1. Think back to a documentary film you have seen. Perhaps it was a segment of a television documentary, such as *60 Minutes*, *Prime Time*, or *Dateline NBC*. Write a couple of paragraphs about the film in which you consider the following questions: What was the subject of the documentary? What was its purpose and its point? What kinds of documentary elements were included, and how effectively were they presented? To what extent did you find the documentary engaging and/or persuasive? Explain.
2. If you haven't seen a feature-length documentary, such as *Sicko*, *Hearts and Minds*, *Nanook of the North*, or the *March of the Penguins*, rent or borrow a DVD copy and watch one of them. Write a one-page summary of the film.

ANIMATED FILMS

Animated films, which bring cartoon characters to life, have long been popular with children, though adults have frequently enjoyed them as well. The first and most important full-length animated films are those produced by Walt Disney, including *Cinderella*, *Snow White*, and *Fantasia*, among many others. The earliest animated films, however, were short cartoons, which have been perennially popular since their inception.

For decades, Disney studios had a virtual monopoly on feature-length animated films. In 2006, Disney purchased competitor Pixar Studios, which has produced, among other animated films, the award-winning *Toy Story*. Disney studios, however, hasn't been idle, having continued to make animated films, including the highly popular *The Lion King*.

Here are a few questions to consider when viewing or writing about an animated film:

Questions for Analyzing Animated Films

- How interesting are the characters? How well do the characters relate to one another?
- How believable are the characters within the context of the film's world? To what extent have the characters been given human, or anthropomorphic, traits? With what effects?
- What kind of voices do the animated characters have? What kinds of physical characteristics have they been given? How convincing do you find these?
- What are the purpose and point of the film? What is its story and what does that story contribute to the film's meaning?

EXERCISES

1. Think back to an animated film you have seen. Perhaps it was a classic Disney film, such as *Bambi, Cinderalla*, or *Snow White and the Seven Dwarfs*. Write a couple of paragraphs about the film in which you consider the following questions: What was the subject of the animation? What was its purpose and its point? How enjoyable did you find the film? Why? Explain.

2. Write a short paper in which you compare one of the classic Disney animated films, or a more recent Disney animated film, such as *The Lion King*, with a film made by Pixar Studios, such as *Toy Story*. Consider the bulleted questions listed above as you compare and contrast the films.

CRITICAL THINKING: *Ancient Rome in Film*

Many films have been made in which Rome has been depicted at different historical stages. Among the most popular is the 2000 movie *Gladiator*, starring Russell Crowe, a film that won a number of major film awards, including Oscars for Best Actor and Best Film.

Why do you think *Gladiator* became a hit? What accounts for its popularity?

To what extent is the film historically accurate? And how would you go about evaluating its historical accuracy?

Would it matter greatly if the plot were fiction while the general spirit of the times was accurately depicted? Explain.

How would you characterize the film's treatment of Commodus, Marcus Aurelius, Maximus, and Lucilla? To what extent have they been portrayed with reasonable historical accuracy?

WRITING ABOUT FILM—THE FILM REVIEW

There are a number of kinds of writing about film. One of the most common is the movie review, which can be found in the newspapers of most cities, as well as in the student newspapers on many college campuses.

Besides the movie review, there are longer articles that discuss the films of a particular director, such as the films of Woody Allen, Federico Fellini, or Steven Spielberg, to suggest a few prominent figures. Another type of film writing describes and analyzes the career of a particular actor, tracing the trajectory of roles he or she plays across a spectrum of films. The more elaborate and detailed reviews of new films by major actors and directors often include analysis of their previous work, as the reviewer situates their current film performance in the larger context of earlier roles and previously directed films.

Theorists of film, like theorists of other arts, philosophize and speculate about the nature of film as a medium, analyzing its technical dimensions, its technological aspects, and its social, economic, and cultural values and contexts.

For our purposes, the movie review provides an occasion to consider films from a number of aspects, without having to introduce specialized terminology about its technology.

In writing a review of a film, you need to watch it carefully, usually more than once. In the process you tend to observe elements and details of the film you might overlook under normal circumstances—situations when you viewed a film simply for pleasure and without the ulterior motive of writing about it.

An Example of a Film Review

The following review is of the 2002 film, *Catch Me If You Can*.

Catch Me If You Can is brisk fun.
by
Peter Rainer

LEONARDO DICAPRIO SHOWS UP AGAIN AS THE chief protagonist of Steven Spielberg's breezily enjoyable but thin *Catch Me If You Can*. It's based on the autobiographical book by Frank Abagnale Jr. about his four-year career in the mid-sixties as a master check forger who, beginning at age 16, also pretended to be a Pan Am co-pilot, a Harvard-trained physician, and a New Orleans attorney. The movie has a bright and colorful look appropriate to sixties pop and an amusing Road Runner-versus-Wile E. Coyote plot that pits Abagnale against dogged, dark-suited FBI agent Carl Hanratty, played with bureaucratic brio by Tom Hanks. We are lulled into believing that this pre-counterculture, pre-Vietnam America was a place where the innocent could more easily be bilked than in our own time. (More likely, the innocence remains; the bilking is just more sophisticated.) The real Abagnale was able to fool people because he was older-looking and prematurely gray, while DiCaprio, although he was 27 when he made the film, looks like a precocious teen. It's difficult to buy the fact that so many people could be taken in by such a stripling, but in every other respect, DiCaprio is a shrewd casting choice: There's an inscrutability to his boyish glamour that makes him something of a cipher; he may look like an open book, but he's not at all easy to read.

Early on, in films like *This Boy's Life* and *Marvin's Room*, DiCaprio had a seething undercurrent that separated him from most fresh-faced juvenile actors. Spielberg doesn't call upon DiCaprio to tap into that undercurrent and go beyond the blithe escapades of a kid con man, and the movie suffers for it. We are, after all, watching a movie about someone who relishes cheating people and treating them as dupes, and although Spielberg and his screenwriter, Jeff Nathanson, are careful to frame most of Frank's victims unsympathetically, we're still left feeling rather queasy. What's missing in Frank is any trace of cruelty or dark guile. Spielberg explains him away as a misguided but well-meaning product of a suburban broken home—Frank's down-on-his-luck-father is hauntingly well played by Christopher Walken—whose scams are meant to reconcile his divorced parents. This is well-tilled Spielbergian turf.

Despite Spielberg's periodic forays into darker realms, he may not have the comprehension of character required to do justice to someone like Frank Abagnale, who, after serving some prison time, was ultimately recruited as a fraud expert by the FBI and today is a highly successful entrepreneur in the security-systems field. (It's as if his ultimate scam was to go straight.) To a lesser degree, and with much more at stake, Spielberg revealed a similar lack of comprehension of the dark side in his presentation of Oskar Schindler in *Schindler's List*, who was also a species of con artist and who was made to seem righteously idealistic. I wish Spielberg hadn't shelved his oft-announced movie project about his boyhood hero Charles Lindbergh; the aviator's pro-Nazi sympathies would have challenged the director's complacencies and stretched him as an artist. For his latest movie, Spielberg can't be faulted for wanting to confect a simple entertainment after the heavy-going *A.I.* and *Minority Report*. The problem is, he's chosen a hero who is far from simple.

Reprinted from *New York*, December 23–30, 2003,
by permission of New York Magazine.

EXERCISE

Select a film you would like to review. It might be a film you have not yet seen; it might be a film you have already viewed but which you think is worth seeing again. If possible, rent the video or DVD of the film so you can replay scenes you would like to analyze and which you might include to illustrate and support the ideas about the film you develop in your review.

Be sure to include the following considerations in your review:

- The type of film
- The main characters and the actors who portray them
- The setting of the film's action
- The name of the director
- An evaluation of the acting performances
- An interpretation of the film's meaning and significance

Perceiving the Arts: Cinema

Like theatre, but without the spontaneity of "live" performers, cinema can confront us with life very nearly as we find it on our streets. On the other hand, through the magic of sophisticated *special effects*, it can take us to new worlds open to no other form of art.

The most familiar and the most easily accessible art form, cinema usually finds acceptance almost without conscious thought, at least in terms of the story line or the star image presented or the basic entertainment value of the product. Yet all these elements come carefully crafted out of editing techniques, camera usage, juxtaposition of image, and structural rhythms, among others. These details of cinematic construction can enhance our film viewing and can raise a film from mere entertainment into the realm of serious art. Bernard Shaw once observed that "details are important; they make comments." Our perception of the details of a film presents challenges because at the same time we search them out, the entertainment elements of the film draw our attention away from the search.

WHAT IS IT?

Cinema is aesthetic communication through the design of time and three-dimensional space compressed into a two-dimensional image. Once the principles of photography had evolved and the mechanics of recording and projecting cinematic images were understood, society was ready for the production of pictures that could move, be presented in color, and eventually talk.

If we examine a strip of film, we will notice that it consists of a series of pictures arranged in order. Each of these pictures, or *frames*, measures about four-fifths of an inch wide and three-fifths of an inch high. If we study the frames in relation to one another, we will see that even though each frame may seem to show exactly the same scene, the position of the objects in the separate frames changes slightly. When this film, which contains sixteen frames per foot of film, runs on a projecting device and passes before a light source at the rate of twenty-four frames per second (sixteen to eighteen frames per second for silent films), the frames printed on it are enlarged through the use of a magnifying lens, projected on a screen, and appear to show movement. However, the motion picture does not really move but only seems to. This results from an optical phenomenon called *persistence of vision*, which according to legend was discovered by the astronomer Ptolemy sometime around the second century C.E. The theory behind persistence of vision maintains that the eye takes a fraction of a second to record an impression of an image and send it to the brain. Once received, the eye retains the impression on the retina for about one-tenth of a second after the actual image has disappeared. The film projector has built into it a device that pulls the film between the light source and a lens in a stop-and-go fashion, with the film pausing long enough at each frame to let the eye take in the picture. Then a shutter on the projector closes, the retina retains the image, and the projection mechanism pulls the film ahead to the next frame. Holes, or

perforations, along the right-hand side of the filmstrip enable the teeth on the gear of the driving mechanism to grasp the film and not only move it along frame by frame but also hold it steady in the gate or slot between the light source and the magnifying lens. This stop-and-go motion gives the impression of continuous movement; if the film did not pause at each frame, the eye would receive only a blurred image.

The motion picture, originally invented as a device for recording and depicting motion, quickly realized this goal. Artists then discovered this machine could also record and present stories—in particular, stories that made use of the unique qualities of the medium of film.

Our formal response to cinema recognizes three basic techniques of presentation: narrative cinema, documentary cinema, and absolute cinema.

NARRATIVE

Narrative or fictional cinema tells a story; in many ways, it uses the technique of theatre. Narrative film follows the rules of literary construction in that it usually begins with expository material, adds levels of complications, builds to a climax, and ends with a resolution of all the plot elements. As in theatre, it portrays personages in the story by professional actors under the guidance of a director; the action of the plot takes place within a setting designed and constructed primarily for the action of the story but that also allows the camera to move freely in photographing the action. Many narrative films are genre films, constructed out of familiar literary styles—the western, the detective story, science fiction—such as *Avatar* (2009; Fig. 11.1)—and the horror story, among others. In these films, the

Figure 11.1 *Still from* Avatar *(2009); Directed and written by James Cameron. Twentieth-Century Fox Film Corporation.*
Courtesy of Newscom.

story elements are so familiar to the audience that it usually knows the outcome of the plot before it begins. The final showdown between the good guy and the bad guy, the destruction of a city by an unstoppable monster, and the identification of the murderer by the detective are all familiar plot elements that have become clichés or stereotypes within the genre; their use fulfills audience expectations. Film versions of popular novels and stories written especially for the medium of the screen are also part of the narrative-cinema form, but because cinema is a major part of the mass-entertainment industry, the narrative presented is usually material that will attract a large audience and thus ensure a profit. In some instances, the "narrative" in narrative film exists merely to serve as a shell for showcasing movie stars.

DOCUMENTARY

Documentary cinema attempts to record actuality using primarily either a sociological or journalistic approach. It normally does not use reenactment by professional actors and often is shot as the event is occurring at the time and place of its occurrence. The film may use a narrative structure, and some of the events may be ordered or compressed for dramatic reasons, but its presentation gives the illusion of reality. The footage shown on the evening television news, television programming concerned with current events or problems, and full coverage either by television or film companies of a worldwide event, such as the Olympics, are all kinds of documentary film. All convey a sense of reality as well as a recording of time and place (example: Leni Riefenstahl [REEF-ehn-shtahl]; http://www.german-way.com/cinema/rief.html).

ABSOLUTE

Absolute or avant garde film exists for its own sake, for its record of movement or form. It does not tell a story, although documentary techniques can be used in some instances. Created neither in the camera nor on location, absolute film is built carefully, piece by piece, on the editing table or through special effects and multiple-printing techniques. It tells no story but exists solely as movement or form. Absolute film rarely runs longer than twelve minutes (one reel) in length, and it usually has no commercial intent; rather, it is meant only as an artistic experience. Narrative or documentary films may contain sections that can be labeled absolute, and these sections can be studied either in or out of the context of the whole film. An example of absolute film is Fernand Léger's (lay-ZHAY) *Ballet Méchanique* (may-kah-NEEK; http://www.english.uiuc.edu/mardorossian/DOCS/films/filmpages/ballet.html). (For a historical perspective on experimental film visit http://search.britannica.com/bcom/eb/article/2/0,5716,119922+6+110698,00.html and http://www.sva.edu/MFJ/.)

HOW IS IT PUT TOGETHER?

EDITING

Artists rarely record cinema in the order of its final presentation. They film it in bits and pieces and put it together after all the photography finishes, as one puts together a jigsaw puzzle or builds a house. The force or strength of the final product depends on the editing process used, the manner in which the director handles the camera and the lighting, and the movement of the actors before the camera. Naturally, the success of a film depends equally on the strength of the story presented and the ability of the writers, actors, directors, and technicians who have worked on the film. However, this level of success depends on the personal taste of the audience and the depth of perception of the individual, and therefore does not lie within the boundaries of this discussion.

Perhaps the greatest difference between cinema and the other arts discussed within this volume remains the use of *plasticity*, the quality of film that enables it to be cut, spliced, and ordered according to the needs of the film and the desires of the filmmaker. If twenty people were presented with all the footage shot of a presidential inauguration and asked to make a film commemorating the event, we would probably see twenty completely different films; each filmmaker would order the event according to his or her own views and artistic ideas. The filmmaker must be able to synthesize a product out of many diverse elements. This concept of plasticity is, then, one of the major advantages of the use of the machine in consort with an art form.

A Question to Ask

What genre does the film represent, and how does it explore the characteristics of the genre?

The editing process, then, creates or builds the film, and within that process exist many ways of meaningfully joining shots and scenes to make a whole. Let's examine some of these basic techniques. The *cut* is simply the joining together of shots during the editing process. A *jump cut* is a cut that breaks the continuity of time by jumping forward from one part of the action to another part that obviously is separated from the first by an interval of time, location, or camera position. It is often used for shock effect or to call attention to a detail, as in commercial advertising on television. The *form cut* cuts from an image in a shot to a different object that has a similar shape or contour; it is used primarily to make a smoother transition from one shot to another. For example, in D. W. Griffith's silent film *Intolerance*, attackers are using a battering ram to smash in the gates of Babylon. The camera shows the circular frontal area of the ram as it advances toward the gate. The scene cuts to a view of a circular shield, which in the framing of the shot reveals exactly the same position as the front view of the ram.

Montage can be considered the most aesthetic use of the cut in film. Handled in two basic ways, first, it acts as an indication of compression or elongation of time, and, second, as a rapid succession of images to illustrate an association of ideas. A series of stills from Léger's *Ballet Méchanique* illustrates how images are juxtaposed to create comparisons. As another example, a couple goes out to spend an evening on the town, dining and dancing. The film then presents a rapid series of cuts of the pair—in a restaurant, then dancing, then driving to another spot, then drinking, and then more dancing. In this way, the audience sees the couple's activities in an abridged manner. Elongation of time can be achieved in the same way. The second use of montage allows the filmmaker to depict complex ideas or draw a metaphor visually. Sergei Eisenstein, the Russian film director, presented a shot in one of his early films of a Russian army officer walking out of the room, his back to the camera and his hands crossed behind him. Eisenstein cuts immediately to a peacock strutting away from the camera and spreading its tail. These two images are juxtaposed, and the audience is allowed to make the association that the officer is as proud as a peacock.

CAMERA VIEWPOINT

Camera position and viewpoint are as important to the structure of film as is the editing process. How the camera is placed and moved can be of great value to filmmakers as an aid in explaining and elaborating on their cinematic ideas. In the earliest days of the silent film, the camera was merely set up in one basic position; the actors moved before it as if they were performing before an audience on a stage in a theater. However, watching an action from one position became dull, and the early filmmakers were forced to move the camera in order to add variety to the film.

A Question to Ask

What kinds of cuts are used most frequently, and how do they affect the overall mood and motion of the film?

Figure 11.2   *Still from an unidentified film. Upward view of men on a sand dune in uniform with rifles.*

The Shot

The *shot* is what the camera records over a particular period of time and forms the basic unit of filmmaking. The *master shot* is a single shot of an entire piece of action, taken to facilitate the assembly of the component shots of which the scene will finally be composed. The *establishing shot* is a long shot introduced at the beginning of a scene to establish the interrelationship of details, a time, or a place, which will be elaborated on in subsequent shots. The *long shot* is a shot taken with the camera a considerable distance from the subject (Fig. 11.2). The *medium shot* is taken nearer to the subject (*First Sunday* [2008], Fig. 11.3). The *close-up* is a shot taken with the camera quite near the subject. A *two-shot* is a close-up of two persons with the camera as near as possible while keeping both subjects within the frame.

A *bridging shot* is a shot inserted in the editing of a scene to cover a brief break in the continuity of the scene.

An important aspect of any shot is its framing, or the amount of open space within the frames. In general, the closer the shot, the more confined the figures seem. We call these *tightly framed*. Longer, loosely framed shots suggest freedom. Julianne Moore makes use of tight framing in *The Prize Winner of Defiance, Ohio* (2005) to suggest nurturing intimacy in her film based on a true story about an Ohio housewife in the 1950s.

Like some pictures and like some forms of theatre, movies can employ open or closed composition in their framing. In closed form films, the shot acts like the proscenium arch in a proscenium theatre . All the information in the shot appears carefully composed and

Figure 11.3 *Still from* First Sunday *(2008). Sony Pictures, directed by David E. Talbert.*
Source: © AF archive/Alamy.

self-contained. In open form film images, the frame is deemphasized, suggesting a temporary masking. Since the dramatic action tends to lead the camera, we have a sense that the camera follows the actors. This creates fluidity of movement. Gillian Anderson, director of *Mrs. Soffel* (1984), uses this technique to add a greater sense of realism to her historical film.

Objectivity

An equally important variable of camera viewpoint consists of whether the scene reflects an objective or subjective viewpoint. The *objective viewpoint* reflects an omnipotent viewer, roughly analogous to the technique of third-person narrative in literature. In this way, filmmakers allow us to watch the action through the eyes of a universal spectator.

However, filmmakers who wish to involve us more deeply in a scene may use the *subjective viewpoint*. They present the scene as if we were actually participating in it, and present the action from the filmmaker's perspective. Analogous to the first-person narrative technique, this technique usually reflects in the films of the more talented directors.

Cutting within the Frame

Directors use cutting within the frame as a method to avoid the editing process. They create it through actor movement, camera movement, or a combination of the two. It allows the scene to progress more smoothly and is used most often on television. In a scene in John Ford's classic, *Stagecoach*, the coach and its passengers have just passed through hostile Indian territory without being attacked; the

D. W. Griffith

D. W. Griffith (1875–1948) was the first giant of the motion picture industry and a genius of film credited with making film an art form. As a director, D. W. Griffith never needed a script. He improvised new ways to use the camera and to cut the celluloid, which redefined the craft for the next generation of directors.

David Lewelyn Wark Griffith was born on January 22, 1875, in Floydsfork, Kentucky, near Louisville. His aristocratic Southern family had been impoverished by the American Civil War, and much of his early education came in a one-room schoolhouse or at home. His father, a former Confederate colonel, told him battle stories that may have affected the tone of Griffith's early films.

When Griffith was seven, his father died and the family moved to Louisville. He quit school at sixteen to work as a bookstore clerk. In the bookstore, he met some actors from a Louisville theatre. This acquaintanceship led to work with amateur theatre groups and to tours with stock companies. He tried playwrighting, but his first play failed on opening night in Washington, D.C. He also attempted writing screenplays, but his first scenario for a motion picture also met with rejection. While acting for New York studios, however, he did sell some scripts for one-reel films, and when the Biograph Company had an opening for a director in 1908, Griffith was hired.

During the five years with Biograph, Griffith introduced or refined all the basic techniques of moviemaking. His innovations in cinematography included the close-up, the fade-in and fade-out, soft focus, high- and low-angle shots, and panning (moving the camera in panoramic long shots). In film editing, he invented the techniques of flashback and crosscutting—interweaving bits of scenes to give an impression of simultaneous action.

Griffith also expanded the horizon of film with social commentary. Of the nearly 500 films he directed or produced, his first full-length work was his most sensational. *The Birth of a Nation* (first shown as *The Clansman* in 1915; see Fig. 11.4) was hailed for its radical technique but condemned for its racism. As a response to censorship of *Birth of a Nation*, he produced *Intolerance* (1916), an epic integrating four separate themes.

After *Intolerance*, Griffith may have turned away from the epic film because of the financial obstacles, but his gifted performers more than made up for this loss, for they were giants in their own right. Among the talented stars he introduced to the industry were Dorothy and Lillian Gish, Mack Sennett, and Lionel Barrymore.

In 1919, Griffith formed a motion picture distribution company called United Artists with Mary Pickford, Charlie Chaplin, and Douglas Fairbanks.

Griffith's stature within the Hollywood hierarchy was one of respect and integrity. He became one of the three lynchpins of the ambitious Triangle Studios, along with Thomas Ince and Mack Sennett.

He died in Hollywood, California, on July 23, 1948.

Figure 11.4 *Still photo from* The Birth of a Nation *(1915). Director D. W. Griffith. View of soldiers out of a bunker.*
Source: EPIC/Album/Newscom.

driver and his passengers all express relief. Ford cuts to a long shot of the coach moving across the desert and *pans*, or follows it, as it moves from right to left on the screen. This movement of the camera suddenly reveals in the foreground, and in close-up, the face of a hostile warrior watching the passage of the coach. In other words, the filmmaker has moved from a long shot to a close-up without the need of the editing process. He has also established a spatial relationship. The movement of the camera and the film is smooth and does not need a cut to complete the sequence.

Cutting within the frame presents a particularly effective means by which a film director can frustrate later attempts to tamper with his or her original product. When transitions occur using this method, it is impossible to cut out or add in material without destroying the rhythm of the scene. Utilization of this technique also means that the acting and action must be flawless and seamless, with no room for error from beginning to end. The effect, of course, creates a smooth structural rhythm in the film, in contrast to inserting close-ups or utilizing jump cuts, for example. In the original production of *Jaws* effective use of cutting within the frame allowed the director, in beach scenes, to move from distant objects off shore to faces in the foreground and, finally, including them both within the same frame. He could also pan across the beach, from foreground to background, seamlessly.

Directors choose to cut or to cut within the frame because the results of each option create psychological overtones that cause responses in the viewer. In the arena scene from *Gladiator* (Dream Works Pictures, 2000), Russell Crowe's gladiator character confronts another gladiator and a tiger. Director Ridley Scott cuts back and forth from Russell Crowe to the tiger and the other gladiator to create suspense. When he combines them all in one shot, however, he produces the maximum sense of danger.

DISSOLVES

During the printing of the film negative, transitional devices can be worked into a scene. They usually indicate the end of one scene and the beginning of another. The camera can cut or jump to the next scene, but the transition can be smoother if the scene fades out into black and the next scene fades in. We call this a *dissolve*. A *lap dissolve* occurs when the fade-out and the fade-in are done simultaneously and the scene momentarily overlaps. A *wipe* is a form of optical transition in which a line moves across the screen, eliminating one shot and revealing the next, much in the way a windshield wiper moves across the windshield of a car. In silent film the transition could also be created by closing or opening the aperture of the lens; we call this process an *iris-out* or an *iris-in*. Writer/Director George Lucas uses the iris-out as a transitional device dramatically in *Star Wars: Episode I, the Phantom Menace*. Although this episode contains fewer evidences of subtextual reference to old films than the original, *Episode IV*, Lucas employs the iris-in/iris-out in such an obvious way in the "prequel" that we think he wants us to remember the device, which was very prominent in early silent film.

Dissolves, then, whether lap dissolves, wipes, or iris-in/iris-out, give the film director and editor a means by which to create a smoother transition between scenes than can occur when they employ cuts. Our task, as participants in the film, remains to develop an awareness of how the director articulates movement from one section to another and how that particular form of articulation contributes to the rhythm and style of the film, overall. We will find, eventually, that we will be able to notice details of

A Question to Ask

What kinds of dissolves appear in the film, and how do they create a response in me?

film composition in passing, without letting them interfere with our enjoyment of the details of the story or mood. In fact, we will find our basic ability to process several layers of perception at the same time quite remarkable and enjoyable.

MOVEMENT

Camera movement also plays a part in film construction. The movement of the camera as well as its position can add variety or impact to a shot or a scene. Even the technique of lens focus can add to the meaning of the scene. If the lens clearly shows both near and distant objects at the same time, the camera uses *depth of focus*. In the beach scenes in *Jaws*, foreground and background show equal focus. In this way, actors can move in the scene without necessitating a change of camera position. Many TV shows photographed before an audience usually use this kind of focus. If the main object of interest appears clearly while the remainder of the scene blurs or appears out of focus, the camera reflects *rack* or *differential focus*. With this technique, the filmmaker can focus the audience's attention on one element within a shot.

Many kinds of physical (as opposed to apparent) camera movement have a bearing on a scene. The *track* is a shot taken as the camera moves in the same direction, at the same speed, and in the same place as the object being photographed. A *pan* rotates the camera horizontally while keeping it fixed vertically. The pan is usually used in enclosed areas, particularly TV studios. The *tilt* is a shot taken while moving the camera vertically or diagonally; it helps add variety to a sequence. A *dolly shot* moves the camera toward or away from the subject. Modern sophisticated lenses can accomplish the same movement by changing the focal length. This negates the need for camera movement and is known as a *zoom shot*.

LIGHTING

Of course, the camera cannot photograph a scene without light, either natural or artificial. Most television productions photographed before a live audience require a flat, general illumination pattern. For close-ups, stronger and more definitively focused lights highlight the features, eliminate shadows, and add a feeling of depth to the shot. Cast shadows or atmospheric lighting (in art, *chiaroscuro*) help to create a mood, particularly in films made without the use of color. Lighting at a particular angle can heighten the feeling of texture, just as an extremely close shot can. These techniques add more visual variety to a sequence.

If natural or outdoor lighting is used and the camera is handheld, an unsteadiness in movement results; this technique and effect, called *cinema veritée* (cih-nay-MAH veh-ree-TAY), along with natural lighting, appears more often in documentary films or in sequences photographed for newsreels or television news programming. It constitutes one of the conventions of current events reporting and adds to the sense of reality necessary for this kind of film recording.

Filmmakers use these techniques and many others to ease some of the technical problems in making a film. They can be used to make the film smoother or more static, depending on the needs of the story line, or to add an element of commentary to the film. One school of cinematic thought believes that camera technique is best when not noticeable; another, more recent way of thinking believes the obviousness of all the technical aspects of film adds meaning to the concept of cinema. In any case, camera technique occurs in every kind of film made and adds variety and commentary, meaning and method, to the shot, the scene, and the film.

HOW DOES IT STIMULATE THE SENSES?

The basic aim of cinema, as with any art, is to involve us in its product, either emotionally or intellectually. Of course, nothing exceeds a good plot with well-written dialogue delivered by trained actors to create interest. But other ways exist in which filmmakers may enhance their final product, techniques that manipulate us toward a deeper involvement or a heightened intellectual response. Figure 11.4 illustrates how angles and shadows within a frame help create a feeling of excitement and variety. An in-depth study of the films of Rosellini, Fellini, Hitchcock, or Bergman may indicate how directors can use some of the technical aspects of film to underline emotions or strengthen a mood or an idea in their films.

Perception is most important in the area of technical detail. We should begin to cultivate the habit of noticing even the tiniest details in a scene, for often these details may add a commentary that we may otherwise miss. For example, in Hitchcock's *Psycho*, when the caretaker of the motel (Tony Perkins) wishes to spy on the guests in cabin 1, he pushes aside a picture that hides a peephole. The picture is a reproduction of *The Rape of the Sabine Women*. Hitchcock's obvious irony emerges. Thus, perception becomes the method through which viewers of film may find its deeper meanings as well as its basic styles.

VIEWPOINT

Very shortly under the heading of "Direct Address," we will discuss the term *camera look*. Sounding similar to the "look" but not at all similar is what has over the years been called "the male gaze" or just "the gaze." It concerns the viewpoint of the film, and that viewpoint plays a significant role in how our senses respond to the film. Louis Giannetti (*Understanding Movies*, page 482) describes the film's viewpoint and "the gaze" as it appears in Mira Nair's film *Vanity Fair* (2004) like this:

> The term ["the gaze"] refers to the voyeuristic aspects of cinema—sneaking furtive glances at the forbidden, the erotic. But because most filmmakers are males, so too is the point of view of the camera: Everyone looks at the action through male eyes. The gaze fixes women in postures that cater to male needs and fantasies rather than allowing women to express their own desires and the full range of their humanity. When the director is a woman, the gaze is often eroticized from a female point of view, offering us fresh perspectives on the battle between the sexes. Becky Sharp, the heroine of Thackeray's nineteenth-century English novel *Vanity Fair*, is a calculating, manipulative social climber, determined to enter the world of the rich and powerful no matter what the cost. This movie version is more sympathetic, more feminist: Becky is portrayed as a shrewd exploiter of the British class system, which is male-dominated, imperialistic, and hostile to women. A gutsy, clever woman like Becky ([Reese] Witherspoon) clearly deserves to triumph over such a rigid and corrupt social system.

CROSSCUTTING

Filmmakers can use many techniques to heighten the feeling they desire their film to convey. The most familiar and most easily identified is that of *crosscutting*. Crosscutting alternates between two separate actions related by theme, mood, or plot but usually occuring within the same period of time. Its most common function creates suspense. Consider this familiar cliché: Pioneers going west in a wagon train are besieged by Indians. The settlers have been able to hold them off, but ammunition is running low. The hero has been able to find a cavalry troop, and they are riding to the rescue. The film alternates between views of the pioneers fighting for their lives and shots of the soldiers galloping to the rescue. The film continues to cut back and forth, the pace of cutting increasing until the sequence builds to a climax—the cavalry arriving in time to save the wagon train. The famous chase scene in *The French Connection*, the final sequences in *Wait Until Dark*, and the sequences of the girl entering the fruit cellar in *Psycho* are built for suspense through techniques of crosscutting.

A more subtle use of crosscutting, *parallel development*, occurs in *The Godfather, Part I.* At the close of that film, Michael Corleone acts as godfather for his sister's son; at the same time his men destroy all his enemies. The film alternates between views of Michael at the religious service and sequences showing violent death.

This parallel construction draws an ironic comparison by juxtaposing actions. By developing the two separate actions, the filmmaker allows us to draw our own inferences and thereby add a deeper meaning to the film.

TENSION BUILDUP AND RELEASE

If the plot of a film is believable, the actors competent, and the director and film editor talented and knowledgeable, a feeling of tension will be built up. If this tension becomes too great, we will seek some sort of release, and an odd-sounding laugh, a sudden noise, or a loud comment from someone else may cause us to laugh, thus breaking the tension and in a sense destroying the atmosphere so carefully created. Wise filmmakers therefore build into their film a *tension release* that deliberately draws laughter from the audience, but at a place in the film

---

A Question of Style

Neorealism

neorealism (nee-oh-REE-uh-lihz-uhm). Post–World War II movement in art, film, and literature. In film, it used hidden cameras and emphasized an objective viewpoint and documentary style. It followed in the tradition of **verismo**, in which superficially naturalistic works are informed by a degree of populism and sentimentality.

The neorealist movement in film began with Roberto Rosselini's *Open City* (1945). It deals with the collaboration of Catholics and Communists in fighting against the Nazi occupation of Rome in World War II. The film has a gritty textural quality that gives it a sense of immediacy, as if it were filmed as a journalistic documentary. Whatever qualities of enhanced realism this characteristic adds to the film came about by pure accident, however. Rossellini could not get good quality film stock, and so he had to use standard newsreel film. Practically the entire movie was shot in actual locations under normal lighting conditions, and, like documentary film, used nonprofessional actors (the exceptions being the leading characters). The plot moves episodically rather than causally and consists of a series of vignettes depicting the reactions of Rome's citizenry to the Nazi occupation. "This is the way things are," said Rossellini in describing the film, and those words became a mantra for neorealist filmmakers.

where they wish them to laugh. This tension release can be a comical way of moving, a gurgle as a car sinks into a swamp, or merely a comic line. It does not have to be too obvious, but it should exist in some manner. After a suspenseful sequence the audience needs to relax; once the tension release does its job, we can be drawn into another suspenseful or exciting situation.

Sometimes, to shock us or maintain our attention, a filmmaker may break a deliberately created pattern or a convention of film. In *Jaws*, each time the shark is about to appear, a four-note musical *motif* plays. We thereby grow to believe we will hear this warning before each appearance, and so we relax. However, toward the end of the film the shark suddenly appears without benefit of the motif, shocking us. From that point until the end of the film we can no longer relax, and our attention is fully engaged.

DIRECT ADDRESS

Direct address represents another method used to draw attention. It constitutes a convention in most films that the actors rarely look at or talk directly to the audience. However, in *Tom Jones*, while Tom and his landlady argue over money, Tom suddenly turns directly to the audience and says, "You saw her take the money." The audience's attention focuses on the screen more strongly than ever after that. This technique has been effectively adapted by television for use in commercial messages. For example, a congenial person looks at the camera (and us) with evident interest and asks if we are feeling tired, run-down, and sluggish. He assumes we are and proceeds to suggest a remedy. In a sense, the aside of nineteenth-century melodrama and the soliloquy of Shakespeare were also ways of directly addressing an audience and drawing them into the performance.

Of course, silent films could not use this type of direct address to the audience; they had only the device of titles. However, some of the silent comedians felt they should have direct contact with their audience, and so they developed a *camera look* as a form of direct address. After an especially destructive moment in his films, Buster Keaton would look directly at the camera, his face immobile, and stare at the audience. When Charlie Chaplin achieved an adroit escape from catastrophe, he might turn toward the camera and wink. Stan Laurel would look at the camera and gesture helplessly (Fig. 11.5), as if to say, "How did all this happen?" Oliver Hardy, after falling into an open manhole, would register disgust directly to the camera and the audience. These represented ways of commenting to the audience and letting them know the comedians knew they were there. Some sound comedies adapted this technique. In the road pictures of Bob Hope and Bing Crosby, both stars, as well as camels, bears, fish, and anyone else who happened to be around, would comment on the film or the action directly to the audience. However, this style may have been equally based on the audience's familiarity with radio programs, in which the performer usually spoke directly to the home audience.

MAGNITUDE AND CONVENTION

In considering the magnitude of a film, we must be aware of the means through which the film communicates. In other words, was the film made for a television showing or for projection in a large screen theatre? Due to the size of the television screen, large panoramas or full-scale action sequences do not translate effectively—they become too condensed. TV films, to be truly effective, should be built around the close-up and around concentrated action and movement because the TV audience is closer to the image than the viewers in

Figure 11.5   You're Darn Tootin' *(1928). A Hal Roach Production for Pathe Films. Director: Edgar Kennedy.*
Source: © Photos 12/Alamy.

a large theater. Scenes of multiple images with complex patterns of movement or scenes of great violence become confusing because of the intimacy of television, and seem more explicit than they really are. On the contrary, when close shots of intimate details are enlarged through projection in a theatre, they may appear ridiculous. The nuance of a slightly raised eyebrow, so effective in the living room, appears either silly or overly dramatic when magnified on a sixty-foot screen. Today's moviemakers, when creating a film, must be aware of how it will appear if translated to the home screen or enlarged in a theatre; their work ought to be designed to accommodate the size of either medium.

In considering a film's magnitude, we must also consider its settings. Gone are the days when all movie sets were constructed like stage settings with large street scenes or studio sets—or even panoramic landscapes. Today much of this can be done by computer imaging. Even traditional animation, employing time-consuming hand-drawn cel images, now largely has given way to computer images created digitally. Animated features, like *Shrek 2* (2004), directed by Andrew Adamson and Vicky Jenson, combine computer animation with heightened (computer-enhanced) reality. The resultant characters and backgrounds have tremendous three-dimensionality and, hence, reality.

The film, as with theatre, has certain conventions or customs that we accept without hesitation. When an exciting chase scene takes place, no one asks the location of the orchestra playing the music which enhances the sequence; we merely accept the background music as part of the totality of the film. We accept a film photographed in black and white as a recording of reality, even though we know the real world has color even though this particular reel world does not. When a performer sings and dances in the rain in the middle of a city street, no member of the audience worries if the orchestra is getting wet or wonders if the performer will be arrested for creating a public spectacle. The conventions of the musical film are equally acceptable to an audience conditioned to accept them.

This consideration of conventions applies especially importantly to the acceptance of the silent film as a form of art. We should not think of the silent film as a sound film without sound but as a separate entity with its own special conventions. These conventions revolve around the methods used to indicate sound and dialogue without actually using them. The exaggerated pantomime and acting styles, the use of titles, character stereotyping, and visual metaphors represent conventions acceptable during the silent era but ludicrous today because of changes in style and taste and improvements in the devices used for recording and projecting film. The silent film recorded action and presented it at a speed of sixteen to eighteen frames per second; when that action screens today on a projector that operates at twenty-four frames per second, the movement becomes too fast and appears jerky and disconnected. However, once we learn to accept these antiquated conventions, we may find the silent film an equally effective form of cinematic art.

STRUCTURE RHYTHM

Much of the effectiveness of a film relies on its success as a form as well as a style. Filmmakers create rhythms and patterns based on the way they choose to tell their stories or that

indicate deeper meanings and relationships. The *structural rhythm* of a film reflects the manner in which the various shots join together and juxtapose with other cinematic images, both visual and aural.

Symbolic images in film range from the very obvious to the extremely subtle, but filmmakers use them all in directing our attention to the ideas inherent in the philosophical approach underlying the film. This use of symbolic elements can be found in such clichés as the hero dressed in white and the villain dressed in black, in the more subtle use of water images in Fellini's *La Dolce Vita* (Lah-DOHL-chay VEE-tah), or even in the presence of an X whenever someone is about to be killed in *Scarface*.

Sometimes, symbolic references can be enhanced by form cutting—for example, cutting directly from the hero's gun to the villain's gun. Or the filmmaker may choose to repeat a familiar image in varying forms, using it as a composer would use a motif in music. Hitchcock's shower sequence in *Psycho* builds around circular images: the shower head, the circular drain in the tub, the mouth open and screaming, and the iris of the unseeing eye. In *Fort Apache*, John Ford uses clouds of dust as a curtain to cover major events; the dust also indicates the ultimate fate of the cavalry troop. Grass, cloud shapes, windblown trees, and patches of color have all been used symbolically and as motifs. Once they perceive such elements, serious students of film will find the deeper meanings of a film more evident and their appreciation of the film heightened.

Another part of structural rhythm is the repetition of certain visual patterns throughout a film. A circular image positioned against a rectangular one, a movement from right to left, an action repeated regularly throughout a sequence—all can become observable patterns or even thematic statements. The silent film made extreme use of thematic

A Question of Style

Symbolism

symbolism (SIHM-buh-lih-zuhm). In visual art, theatre, film, and literature from the late-nineteenth to mid-twentieth centuries. Also known as neo-Romanticism, idealism, or impressionism. It held that truth can be grasped only by intuition, not through the senses or rational thought. Thus, ultimate truths can be suggested only through symbols, which evoke in the audience or reader various states of mind that correspond vaguely with the playwright's or writer's feelings.

Symbols imply relatively clear additional meanings, and the use of symbols occurs frequently in movies. A good example is how Akira Kurosawa, in *The Seven Samurai* (Japan, 1954), uses flames as a changing symbol. The film tells the story of a young samurai warrior and a peasant girl, attracted to each other but separated by strict class distinctions. The two accidentally meet late at night. Kurosawa keeps each of them in separate frames separated by a raging fire that suggests an actual barrier. Their attraction to each other is so strong, however, that they come together. The director places them in the same shot. At this point, the fire continues to symbolize the seemingly insurmountable obstacle between them, but it also shifts to suggest the tremendous passion that consumes them. They come together and Kurosawa moves the fire to the side of the frame where it suggests sexuality. As the scene continues, the couple go inside a hut to make love, and the fire filters through the reeds of the hut's walls stippling their bodies with light. Then the girl's father discovers them, and the fire morphs into a symbol for his moral outrage. As other samurai restrain the father, Kurosawa shows them all washed out by the fire's light. Later, after the young samurai has left the scene in despondence, rain falls, extinguishing the fire.

repetition. In *Intolerance*, D. W. Griffith develops four similar stories simultaneously and continually crosscuts between them. This particular use of form enabled him to develop the idea of the similarity of intolerance throughout the ages. In their silent films, Laurel and Hardy often built up a pattern of "you do this to me and I'll do that to you"; they called it "tit for tat." Their audience would be lulled into expecting this pattern, but at that point the film would present a variation on the familiar theme (a process quite similar to the use of *theme and variation* in musical composition). The unexpected breaking of the pattern would surprise the audience into laughter.

Parallel development can create form and pattern throughout a film. For example, Edwin S. Porter's *The Kleptomaniac* alternates between two stories: a wealthy woman caught shoplifting a piece of jewelry, and a poor woman who steals a loaf of bread. Each sequence alternately shows crime, arrest, and punishment; the wealthy woman's husband bribes the judge to let her off; the poor woman goes to jail. Porter's final shot shows the statue of justice holding her scales, one weighted down with a bag of gold. Her blindfold is raised over one eye, which is looking at the money. In this case, as in others, the form is the film.

AUDIO TECHNIQUES

When sound films became practicable, filmmakers found many ways of using the audio track, in addition to just recording dialogue. This track could be used as symbolism, as a motif that reinforced the emotional quality of a scene, or for stronger emphasis or structural rhythm.

Some filmmakers believe a more realistic feeling can be created if the film is cut rather than dissolved. They feel that cutting abruptly from scene to scene gives the film a staccato rhythm that in turn augments the reality they hope to achieve. A dissolve, they think, creates a slower pace and tends to make the film *legato* and thus more romantic. If the abrupt cutting style is done to the beat of the soundtrack, a pulsating rhythm is created for the film sequence; this in turn communicates to us and adds a sense of urgency to the scene. In Fred Zinnemann's *High Noon*, the sheriff waits for the noon train to arrive. The sequence uses *montage* (mahn-TAHZH), showing the townspeople as well as the sheriff waiting. The shot changes every eight beats of the musical track. As the time approaches noon, the shot changes every four beats. Tension mounts. The feeling of rhythm enlarges by shots of a clock's pendulum swinging to the beat of the soundtrack. Tension continues to build. The train's whistle sounds. A series of rapid cuts of faces turning and looking occurs, but only silence on the soundtrack remains, which serves as a tension release. This last moment of the sequence provides a transition between the music and silence. In other films, the track may shift from music to natural sounds and back to the music again. Or a pattern may arise of natural sound, silence, and a musical track. All depends on the mood and attitude the filmmaker is trying to create. In Hitchcock's films, music often acts as a tension release or an afterthought, as Hitchcock usually relies on the force of his visual elements to create structural rhythm.

Earlier in this chapter, we mentioned the use of motif in *Jaws*. Many films make use of an audio motif to introduce visual elements or convey meaning symbolically. Walt Disney, particularly in his pre-1940 cartoons, often used his soundtrack in this manner. For example, Donald Duck is trying to catch a pesky fly, but the fly always manages to elude him. In desperation, Donald sprays the fly with an insecticide. The fly coughs and falls to the ground. But on the soundtrack we hear an airplane motor coughing and sputtering and finally diving to the ground and crashing. In juxtaposing these different visual and audio elements, Disney is using his track symbolically.

John Ford often underlines sentimental moments in his films by accompanying the dialogue of a sequence with traditional melodies; as the sequence comes to a close, the music swells and then fades away to match the fading out of the scene. In *The Grapes of Wrath*, when Tom Joad says good-bye to his mother, "Red River Valley" plays on a concertina; as Tom walks over the hill, the music becomes louder, and when he disappears from view, it fades out. Throughout this film, this familiar folk song serves as a thematic reference to the Joad's home in Oklahoma and also boosts feelings of nostalgia for some of us. In *She Wore a Yellow Ribbon*, the song of the same name underlines the title of the film, but through the use of different tempos and timbres the mood of the song changes each time it appears. As the cavalry troop rides out of the fort, the song plays in a strong 4/4 meter with a heavy emphasis on the brass; the sequence cuts to the beat of the track. In the graveyard sequences, the same tune plays using strings and reeds in 2/4 time and in a much slower tempo, which makes the song melancholy and sentimental. In the climactic fight sequence in *The Quiet Man*, John Ford cuts to the beat of a sprightly Irish jig, which enriches the comic elements of the scene and plays down the violence.

Nora Ephron, in *Sleepless in Seattle* (1993), uses the soundtrack of her film to juxtapose contemporary and traditional issues by taking classic popular tunes of the 1940s and presenting them as sung by contemporary singers. At other times, old songs are sung by the original singers. In this case, the movie's musical score became a best-selling album (produced by Sony Music).

Our discussion in these last few paragraphs touches only the surface of the techniques and uses of sound in film; of course, directors can use sound in other ways as well as the other elements discussed thus far. But part of the challenge of the film as an art form is our discovery of the varying uses to which film technique can be put, and this in turn enhances further perceptions.

Figure 11.6   *American actor and director Orson Welles (1915–1985) in the film* Citizen Kane, *which he wrote, produced, directed, and acted in. The film is based on the life of newspaper tycoon William Randolph Hurst.*
Source: Getty Images Inc.—Hulton Archive Photos.

Sample Outline and Critical Analysis

The following very brief example illustrates how we can use a few of the terms explained in the chapter to form an outline and then develop a critical analysis of a work of cinema. Here is how that might work regarding Orson Welles's film *Citizen Kane* (1941; see Fig. 11.6).

Outline	Critical Analysis
Genre Narrative (fictional) film	*Citizen Kane* is a narrative (fictional) film that tells the story of a powerful publisher, Charles Foster Kane. The plot progresses chronologically through the events of the central character's life, beginning in childhood.
Camera viewpoint Shots	The shots of the film suggest a variety of styles, particularly angles and lighting of great theatricality. All of the film's shots are extremely careful in their composition. They use deep focus, low-key lighting, long shots, close-ups, and crane shots with numerous special effects. The predominant type of shot, the long shot, gives the film a more theatrical tone. Most of the images of the film are tightly framed in closed form. Welles uses the settings often to enclose the actors in a scene and to suggest that the people are in ways trapped by their environment. Welles also uses the shot to comment on the quality of Kane's marriage. Early on, he includes the couple in the same frame. Later on, they appear in separate frames even though they are seated together at the same table, for example.
Lighting	Over the duration of the film, the quality of the lighting changes from highly keyed at the beginning to very murky and harsh at the end. This change emphasizes the structural rhythm of the film and comments on the nature of Charles Foster Kane's life as it progresses. The effects create startling images due to unnatural angles and contrasts.
Camera movement	Camera movement, like the lighting, changes as the film progresses from Kane's youth to old age. As if to suggest the vitality of youth, the camera moves with agility early in the film. Later, to underscore the stiffness and immobility of old age and, ultimately, death, the camera becomes static.
Audio techniques	The film's soundtrack follows closely all the other aspects of the film's composition, and each shot appears to have its own quality of sound. There seems to be a direct relationship between the visual qualities of the scenes and their aural qualities.

Literature

Reprinted from *Mystery and Manners*, First Edition, edited by Sally Fitzgerald and Robert Fitzgerald (1969), by permission of Farrar, Straus and Giroux.

I UNDERSTAND THAT THIS IS A COURSE CALLED "How the Writer Writes," and that each week you are exposed to a different writer who holds forth on the subject. The only parallel I can think of to this is having the zoo come to you, one animal at a time; and I suspect that what you hear one week from the giraffe is contradicted the next week by the baboon.

My own problem in thinking what I should say to you tonight has been how to interpret such a title as "How the Writer Writes." In the first place, there is no such thing as *the* writer, and I think that if you

don't know that now, you should by the time such a course as this is over. In fact, I predict that it is the one thing you can be absolutely certain of learning.

But there is a widespread curiosity about writers and how they work, and when a writer talks on this subject, there are always misconceptions and mental rubble for him to clear away before he can even begin to see what he wants to talk about. I am not, of course, as innocent as I look. I know well enough that very few people who are supposedly interested in writing are interested in writing well. They are interested in publishing something, and if possible in making a "killing." They are interested in being a writer, not in writing. They are interested in seeing their names at the top of something printed, it matters not what. And they seem to feel that this can be accomplished by learning certain things about working habits and about markets and about what subjects are currently acceptable.

If this is what you are interested in, I am not going to be of much use to you. I feel that the external habits of the writer will be guided by his. common sense or his lack of it and by his personal circumstances; and that these will seldom be alike in two cases. What interests the serious writer is not external habits but what Maritain calls, "the habit of art"; and he explains that "habit" in this sense means a certain quality or virtue of the mind. The scientist has the habit of science; the artist, the habit of art.

Now I'd better stop here and explain how I'm using the word *art*. Art is a word that immediately scares people off, as being a little too grand. But all I mean by art is writing something that is valuable in itself and that works in itself. The basis of art is truth, both in matter and in mode. The person who aims after art in his work aims after truth, in an imaginative sense, no more and no less. St. Thomas said that the artist is concerned with the good of that which is made; and that will have to be the basis of my few words on the subject of fiction.

Now you'll see that this kind of approach eliminates many things from the discussion. It eliminates any concern with the motivation of the writer except as this finds its place inside the work. It also eliminates any concern with the reader in his market sense. It also eliminates that tedious controversy that always rages between people who

declare that they write to express themselves and those who declare that they write to fill their pocketbooks, if possible.

In this connection I always think of Henry James. I know of no writer who was hotter after the dollar than James was, or who was more of a conscientious artist. It is true, I think, that these are times when the financial rewards for sorry writing are much greater than those for good writing. There are certain cases in which, if you can only learn to write poorly enough, you can make a great deal of money. But it is not true that if you write well, you won't get published at all. It is true that if you want to write well and live well at the same time, you'd better arrange to inherit money or marry a stockbroker or a rich woman who can operate a typewriter. In any case, whether you write to make money or to express your soul or to insure civil rights or to irritate your grandmother will be a matter for you and your analyst, and the point of departure for this discussion will be the good of the written work.

The kind of written work I'm going to talk about is story-writing, because that's the only kind I know anything about. I'll call any length of fiction a story, whether it be a novel or a shorter piece, and I'll call anything a story in which specific characters and events influence each other to form a meaningful narrative. I find that most people know what a story is until they sit down to write one. Then they find themselves writing a sketch with an essay woven through it, or an essay with a sketch woven through it, or an editorial with a character in it, or a case history with a moral, or some other mongrel thing. When they realize that they aren't writing stories, they decide that the remedy for this is to learn something that they refer to as the "technique of the short story" or "the technique of the novel." Technique in the minds of many is something rigid, something like a formula that you impose on the material; but in the best stories it is something organic, something that grows out of the material, and this being the case, it is different for every story of any account that has ever been written.

I think we have to begin thinking about stories at a much more fundamental level, so I want to talk about one quality of fiction which I think is its least common denominator—the fact that it is concrete—and about a few of the qualities that follow from this. We will be concerned in this with the reader in his fundamental human sense, because the nature of fiction is in large measure determined by the nature of our perceptive apparatus. The beginning of human knowledge is through the senses, and the fiction writer begins where human perception begins. He appeals through the senses, and you cannot appeal to the senses with abstractions. It is a good deal easier for most people to state an abstract idea than to describe and thus re-create some object that they actually see. But the world of the fiction writer is full of matter, and this is what the beginning fiction writers are very loath to create. They are concerned primarily with unfleshed ideas and emotions. They are apt to be re-formers and to want to write because they are possessed not by a story but by the bare bones of some abstract notion. They are conscious of problems, not of people, of questions and issues, not of the texture of existence, of case histories and of everything that has a sociological smack, instead of with all those concrete details of life that make actual the mystery of our position on earth.

The Manicheans separated spirit and matter. To them all material things were evil.

They sought pure spirit and tried to approach the infinite directly without any mediation of matter. This is also pretty much the modern spirit, and for the sensibility infected with it, fiction is hard if not impossible to write because fiction is so very much an incarnational art.

One of the most common and saddest spectacles is that of a person of really fine sensibility and acute psychological perception trying to write fiction by using these qualities alone. This type of writer will put down one intensely emotional or keenly perceptive sentence after the other, and the result will be complete dullness. The fact is that the materials of the fiction writer are the humblest. Fiction is about everything human and we are made out of dust, and if you scorn getting yourself dusty, then you shouldn't try to write fiction. It's not a grand enough job for you.

Now when the fiction writer finally gets this idea through his head and into his habits, he begins to realize what a job of heavy labor the writing of fiction is. A lady who writes, and whom I admire very much, wrote me that she had learned from Flaubert that it takes at least three activated sensuous strokes to make an object real; and she believes that this is connected with our having five senses. If you're deprived of any of them, you're in a bad way, but if you're deprived of more than two at once, you almost aren't present.

All the sentences in *Madame Bovary* could be examined with wonder, but there is one in particular that always stops me in admiration. Flaubert has just shown us Emma at the piano with Charles watching her. He says, "She struck the notes with aplomb and ran from top to bottom of the keyboard without a break. Thus shaken up, the old instrument, whose strings buzzed, could be heard at the other end of the village when the window was open, and often the bailiff's clerk, passing along the highroad, bareheaded and in list slippers, stopped to listen, his sheet of paper in his hand."

The more you look at a sentence like that, the more you can learn from it. At one end of it, we are with Emma and this very solid instrument "whose strings buzzed," and at the other end of it we are across the village with this very concrete clerk in his list slippers. With regard to what happens to Emma in the rest of the novel, we may think that it makes no difference that the instrument has buzzing strings or that the clerk wears list slippers and has a piece of paper in his hand, but Flaubert had to create a believable village to put Emma in. It's always necessary to remember that the fiction writer is much less *immediately* concerned with grand ideas and bristling emotions than he is with putting list slippers on clerks.

Now of course this is something that some people learn only to abuse. This is one reason that strict naturalism is a dead end in fiction. In a strictly naturalistic work the detail is there because it is natural to life, not because it is natural to the work. In a work of art we can be extremely literal, without being in the least naturalistic. Art is selective, and its truthfulness is the truthfulness of the essential that creates movement.

The novel works by a slower accumulation of detail than the short story does. The short story requires more drastic procedures than the novel because more has to be accomplished in less space. The details have to carry more immediate weight. In good fiction, certain of the details will tend to accumulate meaning from the story itself, and when this happens, they become symbolic in their action.

Now the word *symbol* scares a good many people off, just as the word *art* does.

They seem to feel that a symbol is some mysterious thing put in arbitrarily by the writer to frighten the common reader—sort of a literary Masonic grip that is only for the initiated. They seem to think that it is a way of saying something that you aren't actually saying, and so if they can be got to read a reputedly symbolic work at all, they approach it as if it were a problem in algebra. Find *x*. And when they do find or think they find this abstraction, *x*, then they go off with an elaborate sense of satisfaction and the notion that they have "understood" the story. Many students confuse the *process* of understanding a thing with understanding it.

I think that for the fiction writer himself, symbols are something he uses simply as a matter of course. You might say that these are details that, while having their essential place in the literal level of the story, operate in depth as well as on the surface, increasing the story in every direction.

I think the way to read a book is always to see what happens, but in a good novel, more always happens than we are able to take in at once, more happens than meets the eye. The mind is led on by what it sees into the greater depths that the book's symbols naturally suggest. This is what is meant when critics say that a novel operates on several levels. The truer the symbol, the deeper it leads you, the more meaning it opens up. To take an example from my own book, *Wise Blood*, the hero's rat-colored automobile is his pulpit and his coffin as well as something he thinks of as a means of escape. He is mistaken in thinking that it is a means of escape, of course, and does not really escape his predicament until the car is destroyed by the patrolman. The car is a kind of death-in-life symbol, as his blindness is a life-in-death symbol. The fact that these meanings are there makes the book significant. The reader may not see them but they have their effect on him nonetheless. This is the way the modern novelist sinks, or hides, his theme.

The kind of vision the fiction writer needs to have, or to develop, in order to increase the meaning of his story is called anagogical vision, and that is the kind of vision that is able to see different levels of reality in one image or one situation. The medieval commentators on Scripture found three kinds of meaning in the literal level of the sacred text: one they called allegorical, in which one fact pointed to another; one they called tropological, or moral, which had to do with what should be done; and one they called anagogical, which had to do with the Divine life and our participation in it. Although this was a method applied to biblical exegesis, it was also an attitude toward all of creation, and a way of reading nature which included most possibilities, and I think it is this enlarged view of the human scene that the fiction writer has to cultivate if he is ever going to write stories that have any chance of becoming a permanent part of our literature. It seems to be a paradox that the larger and more complex the personal view, the easier it is to compress it into fiction.

People have a habit of saying, "What is the theme of your story?" and they expect you to give them a statement: "The theme of my story is the economic pressure of the machine on the middle class"—or some such absurdity. And when they've got a statement like that, they go off happy and feel it is no longer necessary to read the story.

Some people have the notion that you read the story and then climb out of it into the meaning, but for the fiction writer himself the whole story is the meaning, because it is an experience, not an abstraction.

Now the second common characteristic of fiction follows from this, and it is that fiction is presented in such a way that the reader has the sense that it is unfolding around him. This doesn't mean he has to identify himself with the character or feel compassion for the character or anything like that. It just means that fiction has to be largely presented rather than re-ported. Another way to say it is that though fiction is a narrative art, it relies heavily on the element of drama.

The story is not as extreme a form of drama as the play, but if you know anything about the history of the novel, you know that the novel as an art form has developed in the direction of dramatic unity.

The major difference between the novel as written in the eighteenth century and the novel as we usually find it today is the disappearance from it of the author. Fielding, for example, was everywhere in his own work, calling the reader's attention to this point and that, directing him to give his special attention here or there, clarifying this and that incident for him so that he couldn't possibly miss the point. The Victorian novelists did this, too. They were always coming in, explaining and psychologizing about their characters. But along about the time of Henry James, the author began to tell his story in a different way. He began to let it come through the minds and eyes of the characters themselves, and he sat behind the scenes, apparently disinterested. By the time we get to James Joyce, the author is nowhere to be found in the book. The reader is on his own, floundering around in the thoughts of various unsavory characters. He finds himself in the middle of a world apparently without comment.

But it is from the kind of world the writer creates, from the kind of character and detail he invests it with, that a reader can find the intellectual meaning of a book. Once this is found, however, it cannot be drained off and used as a substitute for the book. As the late John Peale Bishop said:

"You can't say Cézanne painted apples and a tablecloth and have said what Cézanne painted." The novelist makes his statements by selection, and if he is any good, he selects every word for a reason, every detail for a reason, every incident for a reason, and arranges them in a certain time-sequence for a reason. He demonstrates something that cannot possibly be demonstrated any other way than with a whole novel.

Art forms evolve until they reach their ultimate perfection, or until they reach some state of petrification, or until some new element is grafted on and a new art form made. But however the past of fiction has been or however the future will be, the present state of the case is that a piece of fiction must be very much a self-contained dramatic unit.

This means that it must carry its meaning inside it. It means that any abstractly expressed compassion or piety or morality in a piece of fiction is only a statement added to it. It means that you can't make an inadequate dramatic action complete by putting a statement of meaning on the end of it or in the middle of it or at the beginning of it. It means that when you write fiction you are speaking *with* character and action, not *about* character and action. The writer's moral sense must coincide with his dramatic sense.

It's said that when Henry James received a manuscript that he didn't like, he would return it with the comment, "You have chosen a good subject and are treating it in a straightforward manner." This usually pleased the person getting the manuscript back, but it was the worst thing that James could think of to say, for he knew, better than anybody else, that the straightforward manner is seldom equal to the complications of the good subject. There may never be anything new to say, but there is always a new way to say it, and since, in art, the way of saying a thing becomes a part of what is said, every work of art is unique and requires fresh attention.

It's always wrong of course to say that you can't do this or you can't do that in fiction. You can do anything you can get away with, but nobody has ever gotten away with much.

I believe that it takes a rather different type of disposition to write novels than to write short stories, granted that both require fundamentally fictional talents. I have a friend who writes both, and she says that when she stops a novel to work on short stories, she feels as if she has just left a dark wood to be set upon by wolves. The novel is a more diffused form and more suited to those who like to linger along the way; it also requires a more massive energy. For those of us who want to get the agony over in a hurry, the novel is a burden and a pain. But no matter which fictional form you are using, you are writing a story, and in a story something has to happen. A perception is not a story, and no amount of sensitivity can make a story-writer out of you if you just plain don't have a gift for telling a story.

But there's a certain grain of stupidity that the writer of fiction can hardly do without, and this is the quality of having to stare, of not getting the point at once. The longer you look at one object, the more of the world you see in it; and it's well to remember that the serious fiction writer always writes about the whole world, no matter how limited his particular scene. For him, the bomb that was dropped on Hiroshima affects life on the Oconee River, and there's not anything he can do about it.

People are always complaining that the modern novelist has no hope and that the picture he paints of the world is unbearable. The only answer to this is that people without hope do not write novels. Writing a novel is a terrible experience, during which the hair often falls out and the teeth decay. I'm always highly irritated by people who imply that writing fiction is an escape from reality. It is a plunge into reality and it's very shocking to the system. If the novelist is not sustained by a hope of money, then he must be sustained by a hope of salvation, or he simply won't survive the ordeal.

People without hope not only don't write novels, but what is more to the point, they don't read them. They don't take long looks at anything, because they lack the courage. The way to despair is to refuse to have any kind of experience, and the novel, of course, is a way to have experience. The lady who only read books that improved her mind was taking a safe course—and a hopeless one. She'll never know whether her mind is improved or not, but should she ever, by some mistake, read a great novel, she'll know mighty well that something is happening to her.

A good many people have the notion that nothing happens in modern fiction and that nothing is supposed to happen, that it is the style now to write a story in which nothing happens. Actually, I think more happens in modern fiction—with less furor on the surface—than has ever happened in fiction before. A good example of this is a story by Caroline Gordon called "Summer Dust." It's in a collection of her stories called *The Forest of the South*, which is a book that repays study.

"Summer Dust" is divided into four short sections, which don't at first appear to have any relation between them and which are minus any narrative connection. Reading the story is at first rather like standing a foot away from an impressionistic painting, then gradually moving back until it comes into focus. When you reach the right distance, you suddenly see that a world has

been created—and a world in action—and that a complete story has been told, by a wonderful kind of understatement. It has been told more by showing what happens around the story than by touching directly on the story itself.

You may say that this requires such an intelligent and sophisticated reader that it is not worth writing, but I'm rather inclined to think that it is more a false sophistication that prevents people from understanding this kind of story than anything else. Without being naturalistic in the least, a story like "Summer Dust" is actually much closer in form to life than a story that follows a narrative sequence of events.

The type of mind that can understand good fiction is not necessarily the educated mind, but it is at all times the kind of mind that is willing to have its sense of mystery deepened by contact with reality, and its sense of reality deepened by contact with mystery. Fiction should be both canny and uncanny. In a good deal of popular criticism, there is the notion operating that all fiction has to be about the Average Man, and has to depict average ordinary everyday life, that every fiction writer must produce what used to be called "a slice of life." But if life, in that sense, satisfied us, there would be no sense in producing literature at all.

Conrad said that his aim as a fiction writer was to render the highest possible justice to the visible universe. That sounds very grand, but it is really very humble. It means that he subjected himself at all times to the limitations that reality imposed, but that reality for him was not simply coextensive with the visible. He was interested in rendering justice to the visible universe because it suggested an invisible one, and he explained his own intentions as a novelist in this way:

. . . and if the [artist's] conscience is clear, his answer to those who in the fullness of a

wisdom which looks for immediate profit, demand specifically to be edified, consoled, amused; who demand to be promptly improved, or encouraged, or frightened, or shocked or charmed, must run thus: My task which I am trying to achieve is, by the power of the written word, to make you hear, to make you feel—it is, before all, to make you see. That—and no more, and it is everything. If I succeed, you shall find there, according to your deserts, encouragement, consolation, fear, charm, all you demand—and, perhaps, also that glimpse of truth for which you have forgotten to ask.

You may think from all I say that the reason I write is to make the reader see what I see, and that writing fiction is primarily a missionary activity. Let me straighten this out.

Last spring I talked here, and one of the girls asked me, "Miss O'Connor, why do you write?" and I said, "Because I'm good at it," and at once I felt a considerable disapproval in the atmosphere. I felt that this was not thought by the majority to be a high-minded answer; but it was the only answer I could give. I had not been asked why I write the way I do, but why I write at all; and to that question there is only one legitimate answer.

There is no excuse for anyone to write fiction for public consumption unless he has been called to do so by the presence of a gift. It is the nature of fiction not to be good for much unless it is good in itself.

A gift of any kind is a considerable responsibility. It is a mystery in itself, something gratuitous and wholly undeserved, something whose real uses will probably always be hidden from us. Usually the artist has to suffer certain deprivations in order to use his gift with integrity. Art is a virtue of the practical intellect, and the practice of any virtue demands a certain asceticism and a very definite leaving-behind of the niggardly part of the ego. The writer has to judge himself with a stranger's eye and a stranger's severity. The prophet in him has to see the freak. No art is sunk in the self, but rather, in art the self becomes self-forgetful in order to meet the demands of the thing seen and the thing being made.

I think it is usually some form of self-inflation that destroys the free use of a gift. This may be the pride of the reformer or the theorist, or it may only be that simple-minded self-appreciation which uses its own sincerity as a standard of truth. If you have read the very vocal writers from San Francisco, you may have got the impression that the first thing you must do in order to be an artist is to loose yourself from the bonds of reason, and thereafter, anything that rolls off the top of your head will be of great value. Anyone's unrestrained feelings are considered worth listening to because they are unrestrained and because they are feelings.

St. Thomas called art "reason in making." This is a very cold and very beautiful definition, and if it is unpopular today, this is because reason has lost ground among us. As grace and nature have been separated, so imagination and reason have been separated, and this always means an end to art. The artist uses his reason to discover an answering reason in everything he sees. For him, to be reasonable is to find, in the object, in the situation, in the sequence, the spirit which makes it itself. This is not an easy or simple thing to do. It is to intrude upon the timeless, and that is only done by the violence of a single-minded respect for the truth.

It follows from all this that there is no technique that can be discovered and applied to make it possible for one to write. If you go to a school where there are classes in writing, these classes should not be to teach you how to write, but to teach you the limits and possibilities of words and the respect due them. One thing that is always with the writer—no matter how long he has written or how good he is—is the continuing process of learning how to write. As soon as the writer "learns to write," as soon as he knows what he is going to find, and discovers a way to say what he knew all along, or worse still, a way to say nothing, he is finished. If a writer is any good, what he makes will have its source in a realm much larger than that which his conscious mind can encompass and will always be a greater surprise to him than it can ever be to his reader.

I don't know which is worse—to have a bad teacher or no teacher at all. In any case, I believe the teacher's work should be largely negative. He can't put the gift into you, but if he finds it there, he can try to keep it from going in an obviously wrong direction. We can learn how not to write, but this is a discipline that does not simply concern writing itself but concerns the whole intellectual life. A mind cleared of false emotion and false sentiment and egocentricity is going to have at least those roadblocks removed from its path. If you don't think cheaply, then there at least won't be the quality of cheapness in your writing, even though you may not be able to write well. The teacher can try to weed out what is positively bad, and this should be the aim of the whole college. Any discipline can help your writing: logic, mathematics, theology, and of course and particularly drawing. Anything that helps you to see, anything that makes you look. The writer should never be ashamed of staring. There is nothing that doesn't require his attention.

We hear a great deal of lamentation these days about writers having all taken themselves to the colleges and universities where they live decorously instead of going out and getting firsthand information about life. The fact is that anybody who has survived his childhood has enough information about life to last him the rest of his days. If you can't make something out of a little experience, you probably won't be able to make it out of a lot. The writer's business is to contemplate experience, not to be merged in it.

Everywhere I go I'm asked if I think the universities stifle writers. My opinion is that they don't stifle enough of them. There's many a best-seller that could have been prevented by a good teacher. The idea of being a writer attracts a good many shiftless people, those who are merely burdened with poetic feelings or afflicted with sensibility. Granville Hicks, in a recent review of James Jones' novel, quoted Jones as saying, "I was stationed at Hickham Field in Hawaii when I stumbled upon the works of Thomas Wolfe, and his home life seemed so similar to my own, his feelings about himself so similar to mine about myself, that I realized I had been a writer all my life without knowing it or having written." Mr. Hicks goes on to say that Wolfe did a great deal of damage of this sort but that Jones is a particularly appalling example.

Now in every writing class you find people who care nothing about writing, because they think they are already writers by virtue of some experience they've had. It is a fact that if, either by nature or training, these people can learn to write badly enough, they can make a great deal of money, and in a way it seems a shame to deny them this opportunity; but then, unless the college is a trade school, it still has its responsibility to truth, and I believe myself that these people should be stifled with all deliberate speed.

Presuming that the people left have some degree of talent, the question is what can be done for them in a writing class. I believe the teacher's work is largely negative, that it is largely a matter of saying "This doesn't work because . . . " or "This does work because . . . " The *because* is very important. The teacher can help you understand the nature of your medium, and he can guide you in your reading. I don't believe in classes where students criticize each other's manuscripts. Such criticism is generally composed in equal parts of ignorance, flattery, and spite. It's the blind leading the blind, and it can be dangerous. A teacher who tries to impose a way of writing on you can be dangerous too. Fortunately, most teachers I've known were too lazy to do this. In any case, you should beware of those who appear overenergetic.

In the last twenty years the colleges have been emphasizing creative writing to such an extent that you almost feel that any idiot with a nickel's worth of talent can emerge from a writing class able to write a competent story. In fact, so many people can now write competent stories that the short story as a medium is in danger of dying of competence. We want competence, but competence by itself is deadly. What is needed is the vision to go with it, and you do not get this from a writing class.

Theater

Reprinted from *The Essential Theatre,* Tenth Edition (2011), by permission of Cengage Learning.

> Drama assumes an order. If only so that it might have—
> by disrupting that order—a way of surprising.
>
> — Vaclav Havel (playwright and former president of the Czech Republic)

The play is both the typical starting point for a theatrical production and the most common residue of production, because it usually remains intact after its performance ends. It is useful to distinguish the play—the written text—from a theatrical production of it because the same play may serve as a basis for many different productions. A play has greater permanence than it's the artical representations and may come to be considered a literary work. Drama is consequently often taught apart from theatre; many people who read plays have never seen a live theatre performance, and most students get their first glimpse of theatre through reading plays in literature classes. But a play may seem unsatisfactory or puzzling, because it is essentially a blueprint demanding from both reader

143

and performer the imaginative creation of much that is only implied on the printed page. Learning to read, understand, and fill out the play (either in the mind or on the stage) is essential if its power is to be fully realized.

ON READING A PLAY

There are no rules about how one should read a play. Nevertheless, some observations may be helpful to those who are new to play reading. First, one must accept that the ability to read imaginatively and perceptively is a basic skill that everyone needs; without this skill much of human experience is lost, and intellectually we suffer from historical and cultural amnesia.

Because all writers do not express themselves in the same form, all written works cannot be read in the same way. Each form has its own characteristics, and each makes distinctive demands on the reader. We cannot read a play in the same way we read a historical treatise, an essay, a biography, a novel, or a poem. To read a play adequately, we must adjust our minds to the dramatic form. A play is distinctive in part because it is made up primarily of dialogue constructed with great care to convey its intentions and to create the sense of spontaneous speech by characters involved in a developing action. A play is both a highly controlled structure and a simulated reflection of human experience. Consequently; drama requires readers to contribute more than most other forms of fiction do.

Play readers need to pay particular attention to several things:

- Stage directions
- Time and place of the action
- Implied meanings and "subtext"
- Character action and interaction

Novels and short stories often provide their readers narration that continuously describes settings, sounds, and character action, as well as the innermost thoughts and feelings of the characters. Plays do not usually provide such information so directly. Instead, some playwrights use stage directions to clarify their intentions. It has become common for playwrights to use stage directions which state where and when the action is taking place. But whether this information is provided directly or embedded in the dialogue of the characters, the time and place of the action—for a scene or for the play as a whole—may have significant implications. Stage directions may not only situate the action but also suggest things about characters' speech and behaviour since these expressions are often situational. Stage directions may also help to establish the mood and desired atmosphere or even the tone in which the playwright imagines specific lines may be spoken. However, most playwrights primarily convey intentions through dialogue.

In reading a play, we should assume that what is written is what the writer wished to say. But because the dramatist must convey intentions through a likeness of conversation, we must sensitive—as in life—to deeper meanings which may be implied. The term *subtext* is often used to refer to a character's true meaning beneath the surface level of their communication. Readers must not only understand what is explicitly said and done, but they must also be aware of all that is implied. What is left unspoken may in some instances prove even more significant than what is overtly said. Therefore the reader must be especially alert to actions and the nuances of interactions among characters. Although it is not a simple undertaking to inwardly and imaginatively see and hear what a written text suggests, we can become adept with practice. Perhaps the best place to begin is with a look at how plays are constructed and how structure is related to dramatic effectiveness and meaning. (How playwrights function in today's theatre is discussed in Chapter 12.)

DRAMATIC ACTION

Broadly speaking, a play is, as the ancie Greek philosopher Aristotle wrote in *Poetics*, a representation of human beings "in action." By *action* he did not mean mere physical movement. Rather, he was concerned not only with what characters do but also with why they do it. In turn, the actions of the individual characters relate to some question, problem, or theme that forms the central focus, or dramatic action, of the play as a whole.

Francis Fergusson, a twentieth-century American critic, has argued that a dramatic action builds through three steps: purpose, passion, and perception. By *purpose* he means awareness of some desire or goal; by *passion* he means the strength of desire or suffering that makes characters act to fulfil their goals, along with the emotional turmoil they undergo while doing so; and by *perception* he means the understanding that eventually comes from the struggle. In Ibsen's *A Doll's House*, for example, we see Nora attempt desperately to conceal that she has borrowed money without her husband's knowledge, the increasing anguish into which this attempt leads her, and her eventual discovery that her marriage has been a lie based on a misunderstanding of her husband's character.

The range of human motivation and behaviour is so great that no single play can depict more than a small part of the totality. Because each playwright's view of the human condition differs, each drama is in some respects unique. Still, all plays share certain qualities that allow us to draw some conclusions about the characteristics of effective dramatic action. Effective dramatic action

- is complete and self-contained.
- is deliberately shaped.
- has variety.
- engages and maintains interest.
- is internally consistent.

Aristotle stated that a dramatic action should have a beginning, middle, and end. On the surface, this statement seems obvious, but it summarizes a fundamental principle: A dramatic action should be *complete and self-contained* (that is, everything essential for understanding it should be in or implied in the play). If this principle is not observed, the action will probably seem incomplete or unsatisfying. Effective dramatic action is *deliberately shaped* or organized to reveal its purpose and goal and to evoke from the audience specific responses (pity, fear, laughter, ridicule, and so on). Effective dramatic action, in addition to having purpose, must also have *variety* (in story, characterization, idea, mood, spectacle) to avoid monotony. Effective dramatic action *engages and maintains interest*. The situation must be sufficiently compelling to arouse curiosity, the characters interesting enough to awaken sympathy or antipathy, the issues vital enough to provoke concern, or the spectacle and sound novel enough to attract attention. Effective dramatic action is *internally consistent*. Even if the events might be impossible in real life, they should be consistent with the "rules of the game" established within the play. For example, when during the opening speech of Eugene Ionesco's *The Bald Soprano* the clock strikes seventeen times and a character announces that it is nine o'clock, we are warned that in this play we should be prepared for things to deviate from normal modes of perception—and they do. It is consistency within the framework of the particular play, not whether the events would have happened this way in real life, which leads us to accept events in drama as believable.

METHODS OF ORGANIZING DRAMATIC ACTION

A play is composed of incidents organized to accomplish a purpose. This organization directs attention to relationships that create a meaningful pattern. In analysing a play, it is helpful to pinpoint the source of unity; otherwise, the play may seem a collection of unrelated happenings rather than a whole. The most common sources of unity are cause-to-effect arrangement of events, character, and thought. (The following discussion uses a number of plays contained in *Plays for the Theatre* as examples.)

Aristotle's Poetics

Probably no one has exerted greater influence on ideas about the nature of drama, dramatic structure, and dramatic form than the Greek philosopher Aristotle (384–322 B.C.). The son of a physician, he was sent to Athens at the age of eighteen to study at the Academy, the school headed by Plato, another of the great Greek philosophers. Aristotle remained for twenty years, becoming a teacher there. Beginning in 343, he was for the next seven years tutor to the future Alexander the Great. When Alexander succeeded to the throne in 336, Aristotle returned to Athens, where he founded his own school, the Lyceum. When Alexander died in 323, a reaction against those who had been associated with the ruler made it prudent for Aristotle to flee Athens. Aristotle died the next year at the age of sixty-two or sixty-three.

Aristotle was a biologist by training, but he studied and wrote in a number of other fields. His study of drama led to the *Poetics* (c. 335–323), the oldest surviving treatise on drama. After it was rediscovered in the fifteenth century A.D., the *Poetics* came to be considered authoritative on drama, especially tragedy. Although its influence began to decline in the nineteenth century, it continues to be one of the works most frequently referred to in discussion of the nature and structure of drama. It seems likely that only a part of the *Poetics* has survived, because although it divides drama into two basic types—tragedy and comedy—and promises to treat both, it discusses only tragedy at length. While describing tragedy, it outlines several principles of dramatic writing. It recommends the cause-to-effect arrangement of incidents, progressing through complications and resolution, as the most effective means of unifying action. It also considers internal consistency to be the basis of believability. The *Poetics* is too complex to summarize briefly, especially because the meaning of almost every line has been heatedly debated. Because it has been so influential, it is a work with which serious students of drama should be familiar.

The majority of plays from the past are organized through cause-to-effect arrangement of events. This is the organizational principle used in *A Doll's House*. Using this method, in the opening scenes the playwright sets up the necessary conditions—the situation, the desires and motivations of the characters—out of which later events develop. The goals of one character come into conflict with those of another, or two conflicting desires within the same character lead to a crisis. Attempts to surmount the obstacles make up the substance of the play, each scene growing logically out of those that precede it. Any organizational pattern other than cause-to-effect is likely to seem loose, often giving the effect of randomness.

Less often, a dramatist uses a character as the source of unity. Such a play is held together primarily because all of the events focus on one person. Few plays are unified predominantly through character, however, because, to create a sense of purpose, more is required than that all the incidents involve one person. They must also either tell a connected story or embody a theme. Eugene O'Neill's *"The Hairy Ape"* is unified in part through the character of Yank, but mostly through its central theme of humanity's frustrated search for identity in a hostile environment. Similarly, *A Doll's House* gains much of its sense of purpose from Nora Helmer, but the play is organized mainly through the structure of its incidents. Plays with primary emphasis on character are usually biographical, as, for instance, George Stevens Jr.'s recent play about former U.S. Supreme Court Justice Thurgood Marshall.

Many contemporary dramatists organize plays around thought, with scenes linked through a theme or set of ideas. Vogel's *How I Learned to Drive* shows its central character in various moments in the protagonist's life,

moving easily back and forth from one time period to another as they become relevant to her feelings or anxieties. It is organized somewhat like a musical composition, in which a theme or motif is introduced and then elaborated upon in a series of variations; ultimately, these variations fuse to create a vision of human existence and illuminate a central thought.

Although a play usually has one major source of unity, it also uses secondary sources because every play involves a sequence of incidents, uses characters, and implies a theme or set of ideas. Other sources of unity are a dominant mood, visual style, and distinctive use language.

The organization of dramatic action may also be approached through the parts of drama, which, according to Aristotle, are plot, character, thought, diction, music, and spectacle.

PLOT

Plot is often considered merely the summary of a play's incidents, but it also refers to the organization of all the elements into a meaningful pattern. Thus plot is the overall structure of a play. The plot of a play may be structured in many different ways, but two of the most common plot structures are *episodic* and *climactic*. Climactic plots normally follow the action in a cause-to-effect manner to its conclusion, and, because they frequently enlist a late point of attack, they are often successful in creating a sense of compression or dramatic tension. Episodic plots jump from one scene to the next, often separated by time or place, without necessarily building cause-to-effect relationships between them. Because episodic plots usually treat some central character or concern over time or through a number of variations, they are often successful in creating a broad perspective.

THE BEGINNING

The beginning of a play establishes some or all of these: the place, the situation, the characters, the mood, the theme, and the internal logic (the rules of the game) that will be followed. Viewing a play is like coming upon previously unknown places and persons. Initially, the novelty may excite interest, but as information about the place and people unfolds, interest either wanes or increases. The playwright is faced with a double problem: to give essential information and at the same time to make the audience want to stay and see more.

The beginning of a play usually involves *exposition*, or the setting forth of information about earlier events, the identity and relationship of the characters, and the present situation. Although exposition is a necessary part of the opening scenes, it is not confined to those scenes because information is gradually revealed throughout most plays. Normally, the storyline of a play is longer than its plot. For example, one may view the story of *Oedipus Rex* as beginning, long before the play starts, with the prophesy that the child of Laius and Jocasta would kill his father and marry his mother. Yet, the play begins long after these events have taken place. This choice, to begin the action late in the storyline (known as a late point of attack) compresses events and creates dramatic tension.

The amount of exposition required about past events is partly determined by the *point of attack*: the moment at which the story is taken up. Shakespeare typically uses an early point of attack (that is, he begins the play near the beginning of the story and tells it chronologically). Thus he needs relatively little exposition. Greek tragic dramatists, on the other hand, use late points, which require that many previous events be summarized for the audience's benefit. Thus Greek tragedies actually show only the final parts of their stories. In *Oedipus Rex*, all of the action seems to take place in one day, but to uncover the truth on which the action turns, we must be told about events that begin before Oedipus' birth. Some modern plays have a late point of attack but show, in flashbacks, events that range through many years.

Playwrights motivate the giving of exposition in many ways. Ibsen, as in *A Doll's House*, frequently introduces a character that has returned after a long absence; questions about happenings while the character was away motivate the giving of background information the audience needs to understand the situation. On the other hand, some plays offer exposition without attempting to make it seem natural. Many of Euripides' Greek tragedies open with a monologue-prologue that Summarizes events up to this time. In a musical play, exposition may be given in song and dance.

In most plays, attention is focused early on a question, potential conflict, or theme. The beginning of such plays includes what may be called an *inciting incident*, an occurrence that sets the main action in motion. In Sophocles' *Oedipus Rex*, a plague is destroying the city of Thebes; the oracle at Delphi declares that the murderer of the former king, Laius, must be found and punished before the plague can end. This is the event (introduced in the prologue) that sets the action in motion.

The inciting incident usually leads directly to a *major dramatic question* around which the play is organized, although this question may change as the play progresses. For example, the question first raised in *Oedipus Rex* is, Will the murderer of Laius be found and the city saved? Later, this question changes as interest shifts to Oedipus' involvement in the crime. *A Doll's House* asks,

Can Nora conceal her criminal act from Torvald, and if not, what will he do?

Not all plays include inciting incidents or clearly identifiable major dramatic questions. All have focal points, nevertheless, frequently a theme or controlling idea around which the action is centered. *How I Learned to Drive* exemplifies this alternative pattern as Li'l Bit seeks to cope with having been sexually abused.

THE MIDDLE

The middle of a play normally consists of rising action composed of a series of *complications*. A complication is any new element that changes the direction of the action—the discovery of new information, for example, or the arrival of a character. The substance of most complications is discovery (any new information of sufficient importance to alter the direction of action). Discoveries may involve objects (a wife discovers in her husband's pocket a weapon of the kind used in a murder), persons (a young man discovers that his rival in love is his father), facts (a young man about to leave home discovers that his mother has cancer), values (a woman discovers that self-esteem is more important than marriage), or self (a man discovers that he has been acting from purely selfish motives when he thought he was acting out of love his children). Each complication normally has a beginning, middle, and end—its own development, climax, and resolution—just as the play as a whole does.

Other means than discoveries can be used to precipitate complications. Natural or mechanical disasters (earthquakes, storms, airplane crashes, automobile accidents) are sometimes used, but these are likely to seem contrived if they resolve the problem (for example, if the villain is killed in an automobile accident and as a result the struggle automatically ends).

The series of complications culminates in the *climax*, the highest point of interest or suspense. It is often accompanied by the *crisis*, the discovery or event that determines the outcome of the action. For example, the title character in *Oedipus Rex* sets out to discover the murderer of Laius; the interest steadily grows as events increasingly focus attention on Oedipus, and the turning point comes when Oedipus realizes that he himself is the guilty person and becomes the pursued rather than the pursuer. Not all plays have a clear-cut series of complications leading to climax and crisis. Nevertheless, usually interest is maintained by the frequent introduction of new elements and an ongoing pattern of tension and relaxation. One way of analysing such plays (and all others as well) is to divide them into beats, or units, the beginnings and endings of which are indicated by shifts in motivation or the introduction of some new element. One can then examine the function of each of these units both at that point in the action and in the overall development of the play.

THE END

The final portion of a play, sometimes referred to as the *resolution* or *denouement* (unravelling or untying), extends from the crisis to the final curtain. It may resolve the conflict, make sense of the various strands of action, answer the questions raised earlier, or solidify the theme. It typically returns the situation to a state of balance and satisfies audience expectations.

Plays may also have *subplots*, in which events or actions of secondary interest are developed, often providing contrast to or commentary on the main plot. In *A Doll's House*, the relationship of Krogstad and Mrs.

Linde contrasts sharply with that of Nora and Torvald. Often a subplot becomes a major factor in resolving the main plot, as in *Hamlet*, when Laertes, a morally upright character, is provoked by the death of his father and the madness of his sister to agree to help the king in his plan to kill Hamlet.

CHARACTER AND CHARACTERIZATION

Character is the primary material from which plots are created, because incidents are developed through the speech and behaviour of dramatic personages. *Characterization* is anything that delineates a person or differentiates that person from others. It operates on four levels:

- Physical or biological—defining gender, age, size, coloration, and general appearance
- Societal—defining economic status, profession or trade, religion, family relationships and all of the factors that place a character in a particular social environment
- Psychological—defining a character's habitual responses, desires, motivation, likes, and dislikes (the inner workings of the character's mind)
- Moral—defining a character's value system (through choice and action, revealing what characters are willing to do to get what they want)

A playwright may emphasize one or more of these levels and may develop many or few traits, depending on *how the character functions in the play*. For example, the audience needs to know very little about a maid who appears only to announce dinner,

whereas the principal characters need to be drawn in considerable depth. Even the major characters in a play may be depicted more through certain levels of characterization than others due to the nature of the play or the playwright's intentions. For example, Sophocles gives only very basic information regarding the physical level of characterization for his characters in *Oedipus Rex*. Because drama most often arises from conflicting desires, the psychological and moral levels of characterization are often the most essential. The moral level is developed most fully in serious plays because it shows what characters actually do when faced with making a difficult choice (as opposed to what they have said they or others should do in such situations). Moral decisions differentiate characters more fully than any other type because deliberating about such decisions causes characters to examine their values and motives, in the process of which their true natures are revealed to themselves and to the audience. (Analyzing Nora in *A Doll's House* or Misha in *Lydia* in terms of the four levels will reveal much about these characters and the plays in which they appear.)

A character is revealed through:
- Descriptions in stage directions, prefaces, or other explanatory material not part of the dialogue
- What the character says
- What others in the play say about the character
- What the character does

Dramatic characters are usually both *typified* and *individualized*. On the one hand, spectators would be unable to relate to a character who was totally unlike any person they had ever known. Therefore characters can usually be placed in one of several large categories of people. On the other hand, audiences may be dissatisfied unless the playwright goes beyond this to give characters individualizing traits that set them apart from other characters of the same type. The most satisfactory dramatic characters are usually easily recognizable types with some unusual or complex qualities.

A playwright may be concerned with making characters *sympathetic* or *unsympathetic*. Normally, sympathetic characters are given major virtues and lesser foibles, whereas the reverse is true of unsympathetic characters. A character that is either completely good or bad is likely to seem unconvincing as a reflection of human behaviour. Acceptability varies, however, with the type of play. Melodrama, for example, oversimplifies human psychology and clearly divides characters into good or evil. Tragedy, on the other hand, normally depicts more complex forces at work both within and without characters and requires greater depth and range of characterization.

THOUGHT

The third basic element of a play is *thought*. Thought includes the themes, arguments, and overall meaning of the action. Thought is present in all plays, even the most lighthearted face, because

- playwrights write from a point of view.
- playwrights react in some respect to the broader social point view from which they emerge—though this reaction may be expressed in many different ways.

A playwright cannot avoid expressing some attitudes because events and characterization always imply some view of human behavior.

Meaning in drama is usually implied rather than stated directly. It is suggested by:

- Character relationships
- Ideas associated with unsympathetic and sympathetic characters
- The conflicts and their resolution
- Spectacle, music, and song

Playwrights often use their characters to advocate a certain line of action, point of view, or specific social reform. Dramatists in different periods have used various devices to project ideas. Greek playwrights made extensive use of the *chorus*, a group representing some segment of society, just as those of later periods employed such devices as *soliloquies*, *asides*, and other forms of statement made directly to the audience. Other tools for projecting meaning are *allegory* and *symbol*. In allegory, characters are personifications of abstract qualities (mercy, greed, and so on), as in the medieval play *Everyman*. A symbol is an object, event, or image that, although meaningful in and of itself, also suggests a concept or set of relationships. In *Lydia*, Ceci's quinceañera dress is a reminder of her and her family's shattered hopes and dreams. The dress serves as a powerful symbol that visually contributes to the play's thought.

Just because plays imply or state meaning, we should not conclude that there is a single correct interpretation for each play. Most plays permit multiple interpretations, as different productions of, and critical essays about, the same play clearly indicate. Nevertheless, each interpretation should be supported by evidence found in the play.

SOUND AND SPECTACLE

Plot, character and thought are the basic subject of drama. To convey these to an audience, playwrights have at their disposal tow mean: sound and spectacle. Sound includes language, music, and other aural effects, spectacle includes the visual elements of a production (the physical appearance and movement of performers, the costumes, scenery, properties, and lighting).

DICTION

Language is the playwright's primary means of expression. When a play is performed, other expressive means (music, sound effects, and spectacle) may be added; but to convey intentions to others, the dramatist depends almost entirely on dialogue and stage directions. Thus language (diction) is the playwright's primary tool.

Diction serves many purposes:

- It imparts information.
- It characterizes.
- It may direct attention to important plot elements.
- It may reveal the themes and ideas of a play.
- It helps to establish tone or mood and internal logic.
- It may be used to establish tempo and rhythm.

The direction of every play, no matter how realistic, is more abstract and formal than that of normal conversation. This is because a dramatist always selects, arranges, and heightens language. In a realist play, although the dialogue is modelled after and may retain the rhythms and basic vocabulary of everyday usage, the characters are usually more articulate and state their ideas and feelings more precisely than their real-life counterparts would.

The dialogue of non-realistic plays (such as Greek and Shakespearean tragedies) deviates markedly from everyday speech. It employs a larger vocabulary, abandons the rhythms of conversation, and makes extensive use of imagery and meter. Other types of nonrealistic plays may emphasize the clichés and repetitiveness of conversation as a means of commenting on the mechanical quality and meaningless exchanges that pass for communication.

The basic criterion for judging diction is its appropriateness to characters, situation, internal logic, and type of play.

MUSIC

Music, as we ordinarily understand the term does not occur in every play. But if the term is extended to include all patterned sound it is an important ingredient in every production, except those wholly silent.

Language has been described as the playwright's principal means of expression. But a play is not fully realized until the performers transform words into sound. The elements of pitch, stress, volume, tempo, duration, and quality convey meaning. For example, though the words of a sentence may remain constant, its meaning can be varied by manipulating emphasis or tone ("You say *he* told her?" as contrasted with "You say he told *her*?" or the differences that result if the tone in the same speech is shifted from joy to sarcasm). Because written language is imprecise in emphasis and tone, actors and directors may interpret a passage in ways the playwright did not intend. The spoken aspect of language also varies in its formal qualities. In some plays, among them *A Doll's House,* it simulates the loose rhythms of everyday speech; in others, such as Shakespeare's *Hamlet,* it is shaped into formalized material patterns.

In addition to the sound of the actors' voices, a play may also use music in the form of incidental songs and background music, or it may use song and instrumental accompaniment as integral structural means, as in musical comedy and opera. Music (especially in combination with lyrics) may serve many functions. It may establish mood, it may characterize, it may suggest ideas, it may compress characterization or exposition (by presenting information, feelings, or motivation in a song), it may lend variety, and it may be pleasurable in itself.

SPECTACLE

Spectacle encompasses all the visual elements of a production; the movement and spatial relations and characters, the lighting, settings, costumes, and properties. Because others normally supply these elements, the playwright does not have full control over them; and because playwright's seldom describe the spectacle precisely, the other theatre artists must carefully study the text and consider all the implications their creative choices may have upon the play's meaning in performance. Similarly, the reader of a play must try to envision the spectacle in order to grasp a play's full power. This is true even of subtle visual signals. The visual image of Nora and Torvald sitting down to have their discussion near the end of *A Doll's House* is a powerful choice by the playwright which focuses our attention on what they say as well as suggesting that this is a rational, rather than flamboyantly emotional, exchange.

Some playwrights give the reader more help than others. Many older plays (including Greek and Shakespearean tragedies) contain almost no stage directions, and most clues to spectacle must be sought in the dialogue. When place or action is important, such plays usually have a character describe them. Beginning in the nineteenth century, when visual elements were given added prominence, stage directions became usual. Since that time, the printed texts of plays have typically included many aids designed to help the reader visualize the action. In evaluating spectacle, the characteristics we should be most concerned with are appropriateness and distinctiveness.

Dramatic structure can best be understood by analysing specific plays. Here is a list of questions useful in that process.

FORM IN DRAMA

Plays are frequently classified according to form: tragedy, comedy, tragicomedy, melodrama, farce, and so on. Considerable emphasis is sometimes placed on understanding the essential qualities of each dramatic form and the proper classification of each play. Since the 1960s concern over dramatic form has lessened, in part because much recent drama defies formal classification. Nevertheless, one cannot read plays without encountering formal labels. Consequently, some understanding of dramatic form is helpful.

Basically, *form* means the shape given to something for a particular purpose A sentence is a form created by words arranged in a particular order to convey a thought. Similarly, a play is a form created by arranging incidents in a particular order to create a dramatic action. Most plays have in common certain formal elements that permit us to recognize them as plays rather than as novels, epic poems, or essays. Still, those works we recognize as plays are not all alike. Critics have divided them into a number of dramatic forms on the basis of certain characteristics, the most important of which are type of action, overall tone, and basic emotional appeals. Throughout much of history, tragedy and comedy have been considered the two basic forms.

TRAGEDY

The oldest known form of drama, tragedy, presents a genuinely serious action and maintains a serious tone throughout, although there may be moments of comic relief. It raises significant issues about the nature of human existence, morality, or human relationships. A tragedy's protago-nist, or leading character, is usually someone who arouses our sympathy and admiration but who encounters disaster through the pursuit of some goal, worthy in itself, that conflicts with another goal or principle. The emotional effect of tragedy is the arousal of a strong empathy for those who strive for integrity and dignity.

Tragedy is a form associated especially with ancient Greece and Elizabethan England. (Two of the world's greatest tragedies, Sophocles' *Oedipus Rex* and Shakespeare's *Hamlet*, are discussed in detail in Chapters 4

Analyzing Plays

Dramatic structure can best be understood by analysing specific plays. Here is a list of questions useful in that process.

1. What are the given circumstances? (Location? Period? Time of day? Socioeconomic environment? Attitudes and relationships of the characters at the beginning of the play? Previous action?) How is this information conveyed?
2. Where in the overall story is the play's point of attack? What sets the dramatic action in motion? How is the action resolved?
3. What is the major conflict, dramatic question, or unifying theme? Are there sub-plots? If so, how is each related to the main plot? How is the dramatic action unified?
4. Are the play's characters typified or individuated? What is each character willing to do to achieve his or her desires?
5. What is the dominant tone of the play? Serious? Comic? Ironic? Is the tone consis-tent throughout or does it change often? How is its tone established?
6. What are the major ideas/themes/implications of the dramatic action? Are there a number of possible interpretations of the play? If so, which seems most valid based on the play's action, characterizations, and other elements?
7. To what extent do the vocabulary, rhythm, and tempo of speeches follow or deviate from everyday colloquial usage? What information is given or implied about second, music, settings, costumes, makeup, and lighting? Is this information significant to the dramatic action? If so, how?
8. For what kind of theatrical space was the play written? What characteristics of the play are explained by the theatrical or dramatic conventions in use at the time the play was written?

Not all of these questions need be answered for every play. Additional questions may be needed for some plays or for specialized interests (to meet the needs of actors, designers, and others) or for atypical plays.

The Possibility of Writing Tragedy Today

Is it still possible to write tragedy? This question has been debated frequently during the past century. Few dramatists since the mid-nineteenth century have called their serious play tragedies, and today, though we still study tragedy and talk about tragic form, when we do so we usually look back to the Greeks or to Shakespeare for our examples. Joseph Wood Krutch, a university professor and critic, argued in his essay "The Tragic Fallacy" that it is impossible to write tragedy in modern times because we consider human beings too petty to be capable of tragic action: "the idea of nobility is inseparable from the ideas of tragedy, which cannot exist without it. . . . [A] tragedy . . . must . . . have a hero, and from the universe as we see it both the Glory of God and the Glory of Man have departed. Our cosmos may be farcical or it may be pathetic but it has not the dignity of tragedy. . . . The death of tragedy is, like the death of love, one of those emotional fatalities as the result of which the human as distinguished from the natural world grows more and more a desert."

Not everyone agrees with Krutch's conclusions. Arthur Miller was driven to offer a different point of view when *Death of a Salesman*, following its original production, became the subject of a lengthy debate over whether it could be considered a "true tragedy." In an essay entitled "Tragedy and the Common Man" Miller responded, "For one reason or another, we are often held to be below tragedy—or tragedy above us. . . . I believe that the common man is as apt a subject for tragedy in its highest sense as kings were. . . . [T]he tragic feeling is evoked in us when we are in the presence of a character who is ready to lay down his life, if need be, to secure one thing—his sense of personal dignity."

and 5, respectively.) Few modern plays have been called tragedies, perhaps because, as some critics have argued, we no longer consider human beings capable of the kind of heroic action associated with the great tragic heroes.

COMEDY

A dramatic form that had its origins in ancient Greece, comedy is based on some deviation from normality in action, character, or though. It must not pose a serious threat, and an "in-fun" tone is usually maintained. Comedy demands that an audience view the situation objectively. Henri Bergson argues that comedy requires "an anesthesia of the heart" because it is difficult to laugh at anything about which we feel deeply. We may find it funny to see a person slip on a banana peel, but if we discover that the person is a close relative who is just recovering from a serious operation, our concern will destroy the laughter. Similarly, we may dislike some things so intensely that we cannot see their ridiculous qualities. Nevertheless, any subject, however trivial or important, can become the subject of comedy if we place it in the right framework and distance ourselves sufficiently from its serious implications. Comedy arouses emotions ranging between joy and scorn, with laughter as their common response.

OTHER FORMS

Not all plays are wholly serious or comic. The two are often intermingled to create mixed effects, as in tragicomedy, a serious play that ends happily. Perhaps the best known of the mixed types is *melodrama*, the favourite form of the nineteenth century and still the dominant form among television dramas dealing with crime and danger. A melodrama develops a temporarily serious action that is initiated and kept in motion by the malicious designs of a villain; a happy resolution is made possible by destroying the villain's power. Melodrama depicts a world in which good and evil are sharply differentiated: there is seldom any question where the audience's sympathies should lie. The appeals are strong and basic, creating a desire to see the "good guys" triumph and the "bad guys" punished. This desire is usually met in a double ending, one outcome for the good, another for the bad. Melodrama is related to tragedy through its serious action and to comedy through its happy ending. It is a popular form, perhaps because it assures audiences that good triumphs over evil.

As mentioned previously, concern for giving formal labels to plays has greatly diminished. Today, many people no longer consider is possible to categorize situations and people precisely. Boundaries have come to seem so fluid that a single event might be viewed almost simultaneously as serious, comic, threatening, or grotesque. Thus tone in contemporary drama may shift rapidly and elements that were previously associated with tragedy or comedy might be inter-mingled or be transformed into their opposites. As a result, the old formal categories have lost much of their significance. But we still need to recognize that each play has a form. It is perhaps best to remember that the form of each play is in some respects unique—no two plays are exactly alike—but that there are sufficient similarities among certain plays to group them into a common category. Whether or not we have precise notions about tragedy, comedy, or other forms, we are aware of distinctions between the serious and the funny, and most of us freely use "tragic," "comic." and "melodramatic" to describe events in the world around us. Basic awareness of dramatic form will be helpful in many of the subsequent discussions in this book.

STYLE IN DRAMA

Even plays of the same form vary considerably. One reason for this variety is *style*. Like form, the word *style* is difficult to define because it has been used to designate many things. Basically, however, style results from a distinctive mode of expression or method of presentation. For example, style may stem from traits attributable to a period, a nation, a movement, or an author. In most periods, the drama of all Western prevailing cultural concepts (religious, philosophical, psychological, economic) and by then-current theatrical conventions. Thus we may speak of an eighteenth-century style. Within a period, national differences permit us to distinguish a French from an English style. Furthermore, the dramas written by neoclassicists have qualities that distinguish them from those written by romantics, expressionists, absurdists, or postmodernists. Finally, the plays of individual authors have distinctive qualities that set them off from the work of all over writers. Thus we may speak of Shakespeare's style.

Style in theatre stems from three basic influences and may be thought of in three basic ways:

- Style seems from assumptions about what is truthful and valuable.

- Style stems from the manner in which a playwright uses the elements of drama.
- Style stems from the manner in which a play is presented.

Dramatists of all movements and periods have sought to convey truthful pictures of humanity, but they have differed widely in their answers to the following questions: What is ultimate truth? Where is it to be found? How can we perceive reality? Some have argued that surface appearances only disguise truth, which is to be found in some inner or spiritual realm. Others have maintained that truth can be discovered only by objective study of things that can be felt, tasted, seen, heard, or smelled. To advocates of the latter view, observable details hold the key to truth; to advocates of the former view, the same details only hide the truth. Although all writers attempt to depict the truth as they see it, the individual playwright's conception of truth is determined by basic temperament and by the culture in which he or she lives.

All dramatists have at their disposal the same basic elements—plot, character, thought, diction, music, and spectacle.

Nevertheless, the work of each playwright is distinctive because each perceives the human condition from a unique point of view, and these perceptions are reflected in situations, characters, and ideas; in manipulation of language; and in suggestions for the use of spectacle. In the process of writing, playwrights set their distinctive stamp (or style) on their plays.

Finally, the directing, acting, scenery, costumes, lighting, and sound used to translate the play from a written text to the stage can each be manipulated in many ways; the distinctive manner in which these elements are handled in a production characterizes its style. Many people are involved in producing a play and have an impact on the production's style. Traditionally, unity is the common artistic goal. Each theatre artist usually seeks to create qualities analogous to those found in the play, and the director then coordinates all of the parts into a unified whole. In recent times, postmodernism has intermingled different styles, although this intermingling may itself be considered a style. Ultimately, style results from the way in which means are adapted to ends.

CHAPTER 8

Philosophy

It is difficult to define philosophy with precision, and the attempt to do so forms an interesting and important part of philosophy itself. Even though we should not expect a pat definition, one way to define philosophy is to see what it is that philosophers do.

Sometimes people use the word *philosophy* to refer in a very general way to a person's overall theory or outlook. For example, you might refer to someone's attitude toward doing business as a "business philosophy" or an individual's general outlook as that person's "philosophy of life." "My philosophy is: honesty is the best policy," a recent advertisement said. Used in this way, the term *philosophy* is a kind of synonym for outlook, or general viewpoint. You will sometimes find philosophers using the term in this general sense, but more is implied by the word than that.

((•• Listen to the **interview:** *Kenneth Knisely* on **MySearchLab.com**

In the minds of others, being philosophical means having a passive attitude, taking life as it comes. For these people, to be philosophical would be to accept things without worrying about them. The ancient Stoics, believing that all things are ultimately rational and orderly, argued for a somewhat similar view, but not all philosophers have adopted a passive attitude that calls for a calm acceptance of the troubles of life.

If you look in the dictionary you will discover that the term *philosophy* is derived from two Greek words that mean "the love of wisdom." Philosophy, then, has something to do with wisdom, but *wisdom* is also a term that a lot of people use without knowing exactly what they mean by it. When the ancient Greek thinkers referred to wisdom, they usually meant the knowledge of fundamental principles and laws, an awareness of that which was basic and unchanging, as opposed to those things that are transitory and changing. Ever since then, the term *philosophy* has taken on something of this meaning and refers to attempts on the part of serious thinkers to get at the basis of things. Not the superficial, trivial details, but the underlying fundamentals. Not how many chemical elements there are, but what matter is in general; not what differentiates Baroque from Romantic music, but what art is in general. Unlike the social scientist who specializes in one small area, such as the initiation rites of a South American tribe, philosophy traditionally looks for principles underlying the whole of art, morality, religion, or reality. Putting these meanings together results in a more satisfactory definition of philosophy—the attempt to provide for oneself an outlook on life based on the discovery of broad, fundamental principles.

RATIONAL REFLECTION: THINKING HARD

First of all, then, philosophy is defined by its attempt to discover the most general and fundamental, underlying principles. But philosophy is also different in its method, a method that can be described as rational reflection. As one contemporary philosopher put it, philosophy is not much different from simply the act of thinking hard about something. Unlike the sciences, philosophy does not discover new empirical facts, but instead reflects on the facts we are already familiar with, or those given to us by the empirical sciences, to see what they lead to and how they all hang together. You can see the connection with the first point about philosophy—that philosophy tries to discover the most fundamental, underlying principles.

((••─ Listen to the **audiobook**: *Bertrand Russell*
on **MySearchLab.com**

From our knowledge of science and our everyday experience, all of us have a great many ideas and opinions before we begin the study of philosophy, for example, about what the world is like and how we come to know it. We also have some opinions, before our first college course in philosophy, about how we ought to live. But by rationally reflecting on this prereflective understanding of things, in philosophy we try to deepen that understanding to see what it implies,what it all adds up to, in short, to see it all in a larger perspective.

Through rational reflection, philosophy offers a means of coming to an understanding of humankind, the world, and our responsibilities in the world. Some of the earliest philosophers inquired into the nature of reality, or the philosophy of nature. Many of their investigations formed the basis of the natural sciences, but there was always a residue of concern that could not be delved into by the natural sciences. For example, what is reality, ultimately? Is it merely matter in continuous motion? Or is reality ultimately more akin to mind and mental processes? Is nature merely a blind and purposeless scheme, or does it exhibit purpose? These and similar questions form the basis of an inquiry known as *metaphysics*.

Metaphysical questions directly lead into questions concerning knowledge. How do we have knowledge? Is it through the five senses alone? Or must the senses be corrected by reasoning and judgment? Which is more reliable, the senses or reason? These concerns are among those of the *theory of knowledge* or *epistemology*. Closely allied with epistemology is the study of correct thinking, known as *logic*. Logic deals with the difference between a valid and an invalid argument, how to spot fallacious reasoning, and how to proceed in reasoning so that the conclusion of an argument is justified by the premises.

Another ongoing concern of philosophy is *ethics,* or the analysis of principles of conduct. What makes an action right or wrong? What is my duty to myself and others? And what principles of action are consistent with my understanding of the nature of human beings? These and other concerns must be looked into before one is in a position to decide about the problems of ethics raised by advances in medicine, where we are faced with difficult decisions on abortion, euthanasia, and the morality of organ transplants and genetic manipulation. When the questions of ethics are broadened to include an entire society, one is concerned with *social and political philosophy* and the problems generated by a desire to live in a well-ordered society.

In general, the philosopher is trained to rationally reflect on how the fundamental questions relate to all human activities. Later we will see how these same philosophical methods can be applied to such specific activities as art, history, education, science, and religion.

THE NORMATIVE FUNCTION OF PHILOSOPHY

So far we have mentioned philosophy's use of the method of rational reflection in its attempt to discover the most general principles underlying everything. Now we add a second characterization. Philosophy is defined by a much deeper concern with normative issues than is found in other subjects. For this reason, philosophy can be viewed as a normative discipline. By *normative* we mean that philosophy often tries to distinguish, in very broad ways, what is from what ought to be. To establish norms, philosophy often appeals to the nature or essence of things. For instance, when a philosopher says that humans are essentially rational, this is not a description of the way people are (because they often act irrationally) but how they ought to be. The philosopher is saying that it is only the rational part of a person that deserves to be called human, because that rational part makes human beings different from animals. And, of course, this normative definition implies normative modes of behavior. That is, some kinds of activities should be encouraged, given this conception of what it means to be human, and other kinds of activities should be discouraged.

((•─Listen to the **podcast:** *John Armstrong* on **MySearchLab.com**

The normative function of philosophy also overlaps philosophers' overriding concern with getting to the heart of things, to uncover the general, underlying principles. When we ask in the broadest sense what something is in general, we are asking for something like a definition, and definitions are usually normative. If we ask "What is education?" or "What is love?" we are asking for a definition of things as they ideally ought to be, and it is in terms of this ideal concept that we judge the way things actually are. If we define education, for example, as learning to use one's mind in the most creative way, then we can use that concept to criticize "educational" institutions as they actually exist, say our schools, for emphasizing rote memory and repetitive conformity. "Why, this is not education at all," we will say, "but only a parody of it." Similarly, if we define love as a kind of mutual concern and caring between people, then we will criticize those activities that some people call love but do not meet that definition, and we will praise those that do.

Here again, philosophy differs sharply from the natural and social sciences, which deliberately avoid any kind of value judgments. Unlike the psychologist or sociologist, who describes what people claim to know, the epistemologist (as the philosopher interested in the theory of knowledge is called) tries to find some general basis for distinguishing genuine from bogus knowledge claims. And rather than describe, as a psychologist might, how people do in fact reason, logicians try to find rules for distinguishing correct from incorrect reasoning. And so in ethics: unlike psychologists, who describe moral attitudes and beliefs as they actually exist, the moral philosopher tries to distinguish correct from incorrect moral thinking and behaving.

In general, then, we can characterize the normative function of philosophy as a concern for establishing, in every major area of philosophy, standards or criteria for correct and incorrect ways of thinking and acting: standards for correct decisions about reality, knowledge, morality, beauty, justice, and so on. The search for these normative criteria is no less important a task for philosophy than is its search for general principles. And in accomplishing both tasks, philosophy is guided by reason and logic. The following illustration summarizes the twin functions of philosophy discussed so far.

Philosophy ── Rational reflection ┬─ General principles philosophy
└─ Normative criteria

To learn what philosophy is, one must begin looking at the actual work of philosophers as they examine particular issues, and this is what we will do in the following chapters. But in this introductory section we offer some general guidelines to direct your progress through the rest of the book.

THE SUBJECT MATTER OF PHILOSOPHY

We have defined philosophy as the use of a rational, reflective method for attempting to get at the most basic underlying principles and to discover normative criteria. But what is the subject matter of philosophy? In principle, any area of human concern can become the subject of philosophical interest. Unlike, say, accounting, philosophy does not have a narrowly restricted subject matter.

Originally philosophers were interested in everything, and much of what the ancient Greek philosophers concerned themselves with would now be classified as physics, zoology, psychology, anthropology, political science, literary criticism, and mathematics. In addition, the ancient philosophers were interested in discovering the principles of reasoning, the nature of beauty in art, the principles that regulate human conduct, the standards for distinguishing just from unjust societies, and even the nature of reality itself.

Philosophy, then, can include a number of things. Which of these is the most important depends on whom you happen to ask. If you ask a philosopher who is concerned with the principles that should govern human actions, you might be told that ethics is the heart of philosophy. On the other hand, a philosopher who is fascinated by the nature and function of language might tell you that the most important task of philosophy is linguistic analysis that dispels the ambiguity and confusion that lurk in our ordinary use of words. A political philosopher might insist that the really important task of philosophy is to discover the principles of social justice. We shall come back later to this question of why different philosophers emphasize different aspects of philosophy.

Notice, however, that the state of affairs in philosophy is not so different from what you might find in physics. Physicists investigate many different areas. Some are concerned with understanding atomic and subatomic reality. Others direct their attention outward to the exploration of space, and they would insist that astrophysics is the real subject matter of physics. Still another area of physics is physical chemistry, which in turn is quite different from the activity that interests physicists who explore the various theories of the origin of the universe—a concern known as cosmology and an activity that used to occupy a good deal of philosophical attention in the past.

Suppose that you ask a physicist which of these varied concerns is really physics. The answer probably would be that they all are the concerns of physics and that each has its place in the overall activity that we call physics. At different times a particular area of physics might be more popular than the others. There are fads in physics, and the same is true of philosophy.

To put this last point more positively, each generation of thinkers raises its own questions, and these may be in part brought to the surface by other events. An upheaval in political affairs may prompt discussion of basic issues in social and political philosophy. Major triumphs of science will give rise to a serious reexamination of knowledge and reality.

In our own time, for example, advances in medical technology have forced philosophers to deal with a wide range of bioethical issues.

The agora, or marketplace, was the setting for the communal life of Athens, including such events as the trial of Socrates. The temple of Hephaestus still overlooks the agora, now a popular archaeological site for visitors to Athens. Photo by David Stewart.

Of the many matters with which philosophers concern themselves, it would be difficult to say that any one is the real task of philosophy or that any one of the various questions dealt with by philosophers today is the most important. What may be most important to you may not seem to be as important to someone else. What one age considers to be of serious philosophical importance may seem to the next generation to be completely trivial. This, in part, explains why it is so difficult to come up with a single definition of philosophy that all philosophers would accept as completely adequate.

CONSTRUCTIVE OR ANALYTICAL?

As philosophy goes about its task of discovering general principles and normative criteria, always using rational reflection as its method, it seems to be faced with what appear, at first, to be two quite different ways of proceeding. The first we will refer to as the *constructive* and the second as the *analytical.*

On the whole it does seem that even though philosophy is not primarily a body of doctrine or a set of beliefs, most philosophy does attempt to find the answers to the basic and important issues in life. We will refer to this as the constructive task of philosophy. Philosophers in general have believed that philosophy is a systematic, rational way (as opposed to a religiously inspired way) of discovering the ultimate, underlying reality of which the ordinary space-time, physical world is only a manifestation. In its constructive role philosophy directs itself to developing a total worldview. For philosophers emphasizing this type of activity, philosophy becomes a kind of superscience. It attempts to answer the most basic, fundamental, important questions of all: What is a person? What is the nature of the world? Why are we here? Some philosophers have even rebelled against the strictly rational and logical way philosophy has traditionally tried to answer these questions and have chosen a more personal and emotional approach. Since we are creatures of emotions and will, any philosophy must include those aspects of the human situation as well as concern for the use of reason.

The view of philosophy as analysis provides a still different approach to the activity of philosophy—one that is not opposed to the constructive role of philosophy but can be seen to serve a supporting function. Take the important question, "What is a human being?" The concept, or idea, of a human being seems to be pretty straightforward, and on one level this question may seem merely silly. Everybody knows what a human being is; so if all that philosophy does is to define a term everyone already knows, then what is the point? It is true that most people can pick out human beings from vegetables and pieces of furniture. But what about a four-month-old fetus in the mother's womb? While the fetus is human in the obvious sense of being of the human genus (as opposed, say, to a bovine or other animal genus), should the fetus be considered a human person? What is at stake here, among other questions, is whether aborting the fetus should be considered an act of murder.

How do we decide such a question? Certainly not by looking at biological facts, because both the pro-life and the pro-choice advocates agree on the facts—that the fetus develops progressively from a fertilized egg to a human infant, that it will die if removed from the mother's womb, and that it will probably live if left there. Agreeing on all these facts, we are still left with the question of how to describe an abortion—as an act of murder or simply as removing an unwanted organism from a female body?

We can see how the analysis of one concept quickly leads to the analysis of another: that of "murder." Although there is a publicly accepted meaning for murder, it is not a precise meaning; the center of the concept may be fixed, but its boundaries are vaguely drawn and hence open to debate. If we take the definition of murder to be "the deliberate act of killing another human person," what do we say about the soldier who deliberately kills another soldier in battle? Or the executioner who carries out an execution? The deliberate bombing of civilian noncombatants? The taking of a life in an act of self-defense? Assisting a terminally ill patient to die with self-chosen dignity? As we analyze each of these concepts we are doing philosophy, although at times we may not be clear about the difference between murder and assisted suicide. It is along these fuzzy borders of ordinary concepts that philosophers battle. If, as you followed the preceding discussion, you said to yourself, "of course abortion is murder, but killing in wartime isn't because the two are totally different," then, as a philosopher, you must say how they are different and why the concept "murder" can apply to the former but not the latter.

Philosophy is therefore probably best characterized as a rational examination or critique of the most basic elements of our everyday experience and beliefs. This helps us see how philosophy as analysis and philosophy as constructive are mutually interwoven. Because the world as we are aware of it is at least partly conceptual in nature (a world that includes murder, abortion, violence), the analysis of our concepts of "murder," "abortion," and "violence" entails analysis of our world. And if philosophy seeks in its constructive mode to develop a world view, then the analysis of concepts is essential for that task.

Given its emphasis on rationally examining the most basic elements of our experience and beliefs, it follows that nothing escapes the light of philosophical criticism, not even the assumptions of philosophers themselves. For this reason there are no absolute starting points in philosophy, and philosophy is continually examining the views of other philosophers and of its own past. This is why any understanding of the nature of philosophy must also include some knowledge of philosophy's history, and that is the topic of the next chapter in this section.

Questions for Discussion

1. In your own words, can you state what philosophy is? What aspects of philosophy do you still find puzzling?

2. Some philosophers have claimed that everybody does philosophy or has a philosophy. Do you think this is true?

3. To clarify in your own mind the normative function of philosophy, give examples of the difference between a descriptive and a normative treatment of a topic such as "honesty" or "fidelity" (or one of your own choosing).

4. What is implied in the definition of philosophy as the "love of wisdom?"

5. Do you think some of the activities of philosophy are more important than others? Explain.

MySearchLab Connections

Watch. Listen. Explore. Read. MySearchLab is designed just for you. Each chapter features a customized study plan to help you learn key concepts and terms. Dynamic visual activities, videos, and readings found in the multimedia library will enhance your learning experience.

Here are a few questions and activities to help you understand this chapter:

1. How do you think Kenneth Knisely would define the word *philosophy*?

   ((•─ **Listen** to the **interview:** *Kenneth Knisely* on **MySearchLab.com**

2. According to Bertrand Russell, what is the value of philosophy?

   ((•─ **Listen** to the **audiobook:** *Bertrand Russell* on **MySearchLab.com**

3. What are a few things that John Armstrong thinks you can do with philosophy? Explain.

   ((•─ **Listen** to the **podcast:** *John Armstrong,* on **MySearchLab.com**

Each chapter features a customized study plan to help you learn and review key concepts and terms.